Souls In The Light Field

Aligning To The Celestial SPARK Of Divine Love

Celestial (re)Codes For The Thirteen Tribes

Barbara Christensen

Be Light Create LLC

Woodinville, WA

Disclaimer : From The Diary Of Woo
Barbara Christensen is the creator of the Woo you are about to read, and is not a medical doctor. The author of the book is not engaged in rendering professional advice or services to the individual reader.

The ideas, procedures, and suggestions contained within this work are not intended as a substitute for consulting with your physician or mental health professional. All matters regarding your health require medical supervision. I shall not be liable or responsible for any loss or damage allegedly arising from any information or suggestions within this book. You, as someone that has reached out to awaken your spiritual energies, are totally and completely responsible for your own health and healthcare.

Barbara Christensen is not an initiated Shaman, but is a shamanic practitioner working with the ancient traditions of many Indigenous cultures. We are being asked at this time to carry that fire, and share it so that we can return to the work of caring for the earth and her beings. These are my personal journeys and the lessons that I have taken each to mean. I am releasing this book with the energy of Saturn as it enters Pisces which is the most impactful shift of our astrological year, with the intention that it becomes a gift, opening you up to the mystery coming from some incredible force larger than ourselves, the cosmos, creation and the deep soul space we call home. As I end each of these sessions, I give grace by saying, "Aho", to the universe. "Aho" is a collective thankfulness and gratitude for both your physical and spiritual participation in the creation of my art, in written word. Thank you, I honor you, and I hope this gives you the spark to spread your own light into the world, Aho.- Barbara xx

For information contact: Barbara Christensen
http://www.BeLightCreate.com
Book Layout © 2017 BookDesignTemplates.com

Souls In The Light Field / Barbara Christensen -- 1st ed.
ISBN   979-8-9872240-2-1

THE CELESTIAL CODE (WRITTEN OUT USING DENIS MOSKOWITZ AND ALEC FINLAY'S NEW CELESTIAL SYMBOLS)

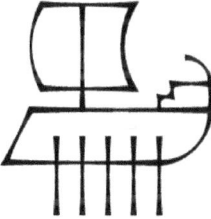

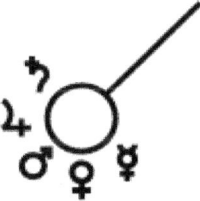

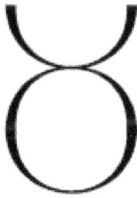

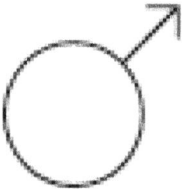

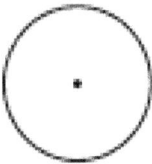

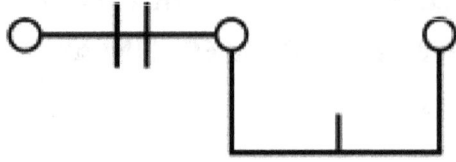

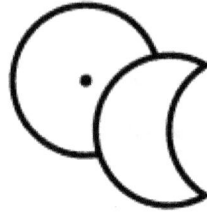

All symbols can be found online in the Public Domain

I dedicate this book to the all of the crazy (woo) beautiful souls that I have met in this light field in life. You've walked with me through the most dramatic shift of this lifetime, and as such we have ascended through the fire together. As fire keepers we are here to create the legacy of energy that will move the light forward for generations. Long after the codes of these stars are gone, and long after the Sun has seeded new light for the future, these codes will remain as the stardust within us all. We are delving into ourselves, and we are finding our way back home. Aho.

"The cosmos is within us. We are made of star-stuff. We are a way for the universe to know itself."

–CARL SAGAN

Contents

CELESTIAL CODES

Some of us are just beginning our journey. Some of us are deep in the portal. This morning I posted the following song quote on Instagram:

"I'll use you as a warning sign
That if you talk enough sense then you'll lose your mind
And I'll use you as a focal point
So I don't lose sight of what I want."
—Found, Amber Run

If you're lucky enough to find the one that is forever the muse to your heart song, the journey however hard shall be like the first kiss again and again.

Love doesn't make sense. Don't let it become practical. Let love be the guide, the muse, the music and the flame, but don't make love quantitative but rather ever expansive in ways one can't imagine.

The divinity that I have experienced in the opening of these codes was profoundly the greatest healing portal. It has unwoven and rewoven the threads of time with and for the collective, but for me it has been what I waited my lifetime for.

Spirit said, "Wake up!", or maybe it was Green Day. Regardless I am awake and ever grateful for the true love I finally feel "in my heart". True love is the love for yourself, and that love allows you to love others independently of the feelings you carry for "you". You of body, you of timing, and you of soul as the Triad of the Golden Ratio that was created as an atomic spark of the Divine. The Divine created you as an extension of oneness, and in this rebirth, you are truly free like the stars that you carry within.

My muse, you led the great Shamans to me so that I could open to the frequency of love. You, decidedly undecided, that opened the gate to the Cosmos so that I could find my true heart and return to it for the embodiment of love.

Know you are loved.
I know I am loved.
Aho
Barbara xx

The codes came to me at a time that I was slowly reorganizing my own cellular structure in more ways than one. Through the journey of body, mind, soul and spirit I found that the connection we have to the closest celestial structures of this Universe, are impacting us at every moment in ways that we cannot even understand fully. We talk about the retrogrades causing havoc on our technology, solar flares as well, and yet I felt that there was something more going on here than we were realizing.

Terrfirma, solid ground, the way we look at reality through the lens of living on a planet that some say is flat, others say is round, but all that matters truly is that it is the solid ground that we walk on in this daily lifetime. Sometimes we are in the one object in the vast universe that allows us to fill that we are firmly planted somewhere safe. As I started working with these codes, I found comfort in knowing that all of this came long before us, and it will remain long after we're gone.

I call this an alignment to love. Love is something that is always within us, yet we all spend our lives seeking that feeling outside of us. As such, we spend a lifetime within the orbit of Planet Earth, and yet we spend a lifetime staring at these stars that seem so far and distant, and yet make up the essence of who we are at a cellular level.

The Thirteen Tribes are both my Zodiac and kundalini planes reference. Ophiuchus, the ninth Zodiac sign, first arrived into my YouTube channel as my muse. I saw Ophiuchus as this spectacular energy that encompassed starseeds, Bluerays, the life container and the collective ascension into the union of love with the one other half of your soul. That can be within ourselves as we have both feminine and masculine energies within, or the union of two divine lovers that were destined to find each other in this life.

All of this came to me at the most divine timing, as I was about to go through my shamanic awakening, which I wrote about in my book, "From The Diary Of Woo". Things happen when they are meant to happen. So even if I am writing about something that happened in the astroplane in 2021, time is fluid and if it resonates with where you are now, and what you need to learn, then take it and let it teach you. If it doesn't make any sense to you, just let it go. This work is my woo, my space to write out the crazy that comes into my dreams, my auric field, and that feels into the quantum reality that I call life. What it means to me, could be something completely different than what comes to mind for you. In my Sacred Space shamanic circle, I like to share my journey, and often relate to what others are experiencing, but that in no way means that it has to be perceived through my life experience. Just like with love, you can love someone that is unrequited and yet that does not diminish your love.

I offer these codes and the videos that I created with some of them as a gift from my sacred journey. I believe there are messages within this work for you, even if all of them are not. You found this at the right time, and the channeling that created it was created for you. You are a spark of light that makes up the unique frequency of this moment. Embrace that, embrace you and I hope that this lands in the heart space of unconditional love for yourself most of all.

Ka'epaoka'āwela, the asteroid that is the "tricky one", was found in November of 2014, when I was considering why I was being called back to the Pacific Northwest. This means something significant to me because this asteroid orbits Jupiter in retrograde. It is significant in the world of Astronomy because it was the first is example of an asteroid in a 1:–1 resonance with a planet. It is not gravitationally bound to the Sun, which is extremely interesting. For a million years it has orbited in retrograde around Jupiter, and they believe It will for another million years before Saturn may come close enough to set it free. That is one long karmic lesson, or spiritual expansion. So, we have but to ask, and the Universe answers.

It also may have originated from the Oort Cloud, where Comet Leonard was proposed to have originated. Or is in retrograde due to its close connection to Nibiru, Planet X, also known as the 'Goblin'. Eventually researchers turned to a differing idea of what they now call, Planet Nine, and yet they are the same idea as the planet that is beyond Neptune.

Neptune is what I see as our higher heart chakra, and it is our closest connection to our own unconditional love. It guides us with the knowing that there is something greater than ourselves, and that is still a drop of the atomic or etheric being of ourselves. I am not here as an astrological professor, or even as a great study of this field. These are just the messages that have come out my channeling or meditative trance, and they are just saying hello, or koé, as they would say in Brazil. What's up? That's what the planets, the stars, and the cosmic dust flying around out there is saying this morning. Like a small part of my DNA comes from Iberia, and perhaps my cousins moved to Brazil, and my closer relatives moved to Sweden, Denmark, Finland, Scotland, Ireland, England, France, etc. We are all still somehow related, and yet we are all something magically different.

It doesn't matter where you come from, and there is no trickery here. No scary spells to be cast by reading these stories. You can use them as fiction, or use them to delve deeper into your own healing journey. When you are done, please reach out and tell me "what's up", and share your discoveries of what it created uniquely with you.

THE DRAGON AWAKENS

O liver, my terrier that is often facilitating energy on the YouTube Channel with me (*@MindsetUnicorn or @OracleOfTheCelestial*), drug me outside this morning and in a moment of rarity I was able to see some stars. The Little Dipper caught my eye as Polaris was so bright. But then there was this other star that seemed to be blinking at me. Well, I thought, this is odd. That star was Thuban, the Axis Mundi. I am told this star was once the Pole Star, the star the Great Pyramid King's chamber was aligned to thousands of years ago. It is also the heart of the universal tree of life. Axis Mundi is where the heavens meet the earth. This is the great crossroads, the opening to the Upper Realm. We are ready to open the next set of lessons through the channeling work that I have used to write all of my books. Thus, I was guided that it was time to start writing the codes.

When I last left you, we were working into the Enlightened Karma, and here we are in a numerological year of 7, the Karmic. Initiated into our inner work, and we were tired. This was a global fatigue, and my heart still aches from the loss that we've all experienced, despite knowing that we choose this path. I was also not even able to fully comprehend that I was initiated into my own karmic purge, and that I was at a great crossroads. Yet here I am, soaring into a new life with barely dry wings. Let's fly into these new codes together.

This crossroads, or center of the tree of all life, is also called the Heart of the Universe. The magical celestial pole where the mystic realms collide. They say this is the place where the Kings become The Emperor (Divine Masculine). Its power is guarded by the Serpent. The serpent is a sacred symbolism of fertility, as well as very special to me as the symbology of Ophiuchus, and our karmic wheel. Just last year, in 2020, we realized that Thuban is not one star but a binary star of two. It has a divine partner, and it is there we find the Divine Feminine. The more we see these binary star systems, the more we are seeing celestial confirmation that this is a symbol of divine union.

I saw this for myself as a confirmation of the channeled messages that came through for the sign of Virgo in the 'Celestial Spark' book. The Serpent will find a greater placement as we move into these newly channeled messages, as we are shedding the past to grow into the future. In the Virgo stories it was told that,

"You know that there is a part of you missing, and depending on if you find yourself feeling wounded in your deep masculine side or your deep feminine side, and then you will act accordingly. This is where your mutable qualities can shift.

You look in a mirror. On one side is your masculine self, on the other side is your feminine self. You feel great sadness in the separation as you long for integration. Divine union within, you now see, is something you truly desire."

I am reminded that we can't see our true alignment until we have worked on our inner child, and collectively we have work to do. The mirroring is just the beginning, and the mirroring was being shown to me that morning.

I had never thought before about seeing the Little Dipper in the upright position before, which means that the Big Dipper is upside down. Their handles extend in opposite directions and are a symbolism of our resistance to balancing our yin and yang. There is an undeniable bond between the feminine and masculine, but also between the grown you and the inner child. You can't be aligned with one without being integrated with the other. I also had never thought about seeing the positions of the constellations from different angles, but that is part of what we are being asked to do. We cannot look at the world through the lens of a hidden child, but healed we can look with wonder.

I went into the journey space with a light stream bubbling like water around me, and beautiful flute music playing in the background. The White Haired Shaman woman appeared and took my hand. We were in a beautiful tropical rainforest and first we were walking, and then running, before walking some more. She stopped and took both of my hands and we did this spiral dance together where we would face towards each other and then turn away without ever letting go completely. Spiral is the symbology of life, the Golden Ratio, the beginning and the ending of everything is ingrained in the spiral. Mother Spider came in and she joined the dance, and then she asked us both to sit.

We sat in a sacred circle together and the shaman started telling us a story of long before our time when the women of the celestial tribes could fly. They controlled the Light, they controlled the stars, but it was a symbiotic relationship and not a control of another's energies. It was symbiotic with the energy field.

She told Mother Spider and I that with the help of Mother Spider's light grids, I could also learn how to fly. This made Mother Spider exceptionally happy. We jumped up and danced again while Mother Spider wove a little of her light webbing around my waist and then crawled across the sky weaving her web. She looked at me and said, "Now fly."

I couldn't fly, I thought. I did a little jump but came firmly back down to the ground, hard. Mother Spider said, "You must believe that you are attached to these light grids more than you believe in the power of gravity." I leapt again and the freedom of flight caught hold, and it was magnificent. I was soaring and dancing across the sky. My old body shed away, and although I could tell that now I was a light body, I was still deeply connected to my human form of body and soul.

The Divine Feminine soaring mythology has been sprinkled throughout the stories passed from generation to generation. She appears as the feathered serpent to me, Icarus, or as she was shown to me as "She who guides us."

MACS J1149+2223 Lensed Star 1, is the farthest individual star ever seen, and she is named Icarus. This bright blue giant star is guiding us to the celestial home we are seeking, and was found in the mouth of the lion, Leo. Icarus is also the name of an asteroid that as I am writing this at the end of 2021, is sitting in the constellation Microscopium, the microscope.

In 2014 there were strange wave-like ripples that were seen coming from this constellation. There was something happening in that year, and it was like a ripple into our relationships, all of the relationships. That was the first nudge from the Universe to get into the right position to quantum leap, but I wasn't ready. Honestly, I can tell you now, with certainty, none of us ever feel truly ready.

There were two Cardinal Grand Crosses in 2014, which can appear like the cross is spinning like a generator and this creates polarities involving building up a tremendous charge. This energy tends to be released through out-of-control bursts, triggering chaos and crisis. I feel like this is what we were seeing, because up to this point, they cannot explain it. I think it was the start of the decade of transition into the New Age of Aquarius.

In the beginning of this universe, the poles were reversed and the Divine Masculine was the keeper of the Earth plane and the Divine Feminine the Goddesses of the Cosmos. As I have shared, every civilization has mythology that incorporates a feminine flying goddess, or goddess of the air. In a cave in France, you can find the Paleolithic painting of the flying goddesses, and the constellations were used by these hunter-gatherers for orientation in space as well as for calculating the seasonal timing.

There was a celestial meeting at the Sacred Circle in the Axis Mundi, the Heart of the Universe. This is where the masculine came to claim their Emperor energy. The one running like bulls in the celestial sky patterns, changing theirselves into pure energy to win the affections of the Divine Feminine. They split in two and the other half moved into the Earth to run like bulls in human form. For the Divine Masculine human form to awaken is not so easy, as the spiritual side is uncertain about entering this season until they are also changed. The Bull was asking to be sacrificed, but fearful to be. Yes, it is true, and yet mostly in the 3D our masculine energy digs in the stubborn heels and gores rather than gives. Unlike the Divine Feminine who had sacrificed themselves in the Buffalo Heart Medicine that I was taught from my shamanic journeys. This I wrote about in, 'From The Diary Of Woo'. I have gone back and reread these books many times, and every time I get a new wave of knowledge from them.

The Divine Feminine came into the meeting and was easily moved to do the same thing. However, they first moved deeper into the earth to connect to the heart of creation before being born into human life. This was their way of allowing themselves to be the programmers of the ascension codes, so that when they came into the role of this new life, they could find their way. As they grew into this new form, they lifted their wings to try to tap into the knowledge of the Heavens in order to keep the codes up to date, and this is why we see mostly Divine Feminine energy in the ascension process to date. The Divine Heart is still looking to access the So Above, and connect it to So Below. The Divine Power is generally still digging into the dirt and trying to gore anything that gets in its way.

The Feminine Shaman in this journey is the other side of the Masculine Shaman that I wrote about for the Virgo dúSa Souls channeled story. This morning all of the information came full circle as Archangel Gabriel came to me and showed me his star, the Star of Gabriel. His star, Errai, will be the new North Star in the future age of Aquarius, and it is also guiding us. You may know this star by another name, Gamma Cephei. From Gabriel's point of view our own Cassiopeia is not a 'W' but acknowledges the Sun and becomes the Serpent. The Incas considered the river Vilcanota, which crosses through the Sacred Valley, to be a reflection of the Milky Way, as a Serpent. I think it will only be a matter of time before we find that there is another matching river out there, as well.

Both Gamma Cephei and Alpha Centauri are believed to be adversely affected by the presence of the stellar companion, as they are binary stars, we now know. They come to play an essential part again and again in these codes. However, they also come to me as being an essential part of this lighting of the celestial field. They are here to spark the flame. This Is the Divine Masculine and Divine Feminine exerting their energy into the Universe. It is a spark that no one can deny once they've felt it. I feel that we are only now in discovery of the opening of these ancient sacred teachings. We are barely tapping into the knowledge that we left for our souls in the light fields. There in the stars, all that we seek is waiting to be discovered.

So, I looked deeper into the stars and they showed me that Kokobiel, who came to me in the last channeling of the *'Celestial Spark'* book, has ignited another birth as the Star of God, splitting an essence of Gabriel into two. We are learning from the star teachers, and the angelic protectors. All things eventually are in the realm of what we call two, so that the mirroring frequency continues aligning to our soul's house. We are not one and two, but we are zero and one.

This morning those messages that I am sharing with you started in the dream sequence where I was in a house of a religious cult. I feel that this was metaphorically speaking about where we are in current days. We are learning through science that the energy flow that has been a part of tribal life since life began, and is measurable and factual. Science is Spirit and spirituality is growing.

Gabriel came to me in this very large building in a complex of buildings, and I was shown his star to guide my awakening. We are all awakening to the complexity of our house of the global community. In as much as we want to believe, it is highly reflected in the changes happening in the house of our soul. Our bodies are rapidly changing and DNA is asking for support to keep up pace. I can understand why Spirit guided me first through the functionality of the body as a machine with nutrition, physicality and natural alternatives, so that we could tap into greater energies with the epigenetic support of these sacred plants. For those that are new to my channeling, I hold a diploma in nutrition, and I am certified in personal training. I am also a Certified Aromatherapist as well as what I call a working Holistic Bio-Energetist.

They brought me to Errai to start teaching me. Errai is a binary pair with the planet that has been named Tadmor. Errai and Tadmor as the approaching North Star, taking over for Polaris A and B, who had caught my eye at the start of this channeled story. I am told all North Stars will only come in pairs going forward. I am not surprised that Errai has come forward as this is a main star in the constellation Cepheus, who is the King, and makes up the constellation outline. The celestial Emperor is starting to show itself to the physical masculine.

You will feel Errai pulling in the sacral chakra as you work on the masculine space within yourself. Tadmor's meaning is the 'place of love' or the "wife" or "maiden of the desert". The orbital time is 900 days, speaking to the working together in harmony. This is what we are being guided to.

The view of the current North Star, Polaris, in Ursa Major, the bear, from Errai appears to be the runes of Feoh (wealth) and Ur (cattle). Very different from what we see from Earth. The celestial view of the Divine Masculine is that of already being the Emperor, but it is the biggest struggle I see in the Divine Masculine today, as they are still chasing transactional roles.

In my journey with the bear, I started the journey in a red world, Errai, but soon moved into a land where I was the Sun. It would take almost a year for me to move into how important this would be to our evolutionary cosmology.

The Sun is seen as the Masculine of the Cosmos after they had the meeting of the Axis Mundi. There I saw a woman dancing on the dry desert in a rain dance trying to break through the dimensional space. I think this was Tadmor, coming in as the Maiden, the Divine Feminine energy. I became the woman and we went up a mountain into a cave. A large brown bear came up from behind us and I laid down to face my end, but instead the bear walked in front of me. The bear laid down into my body and I became the bear.

It was something of magic that happened after my expansion with Jupiter, and I started working with the gift of the Shapeshifter. In such, I can take on the embodiment of the animal totem to gain deeper wisdom through a deeply shamanic practice.

Together as one, we danced, and as we came out of the cave the rain started to come. I am ready to move into the world as the bear medicine as the rains have cleansed the path forward. Divine Masculine, the path forward is now clear. The ripples are calming and you may open to your emotional transformation. That, I am told, may be a return to the cross to see yourself as you originally were, rather than in a Earth School body.

I was then taken into the Upper Realm with fire, and was inside of Errai again. Soon I could see the Divine Masculine, working on a stick of wood, carving it into a weapon. The Divine Feminine energy watched as Sagittarius galloped by, shooting an arrow to follow into the realm where the healing would begin. This space was in the heart of the Divine Masculine.

The Divine Masculine touched the hair of the Divine Feminine, and smiled, still holding the stick, but no longer working on it as a weapon. The Divine Feminine asked what it was that was causing the Divine Masculine to work on this weaponry, and they answered with one thing - fire. There is a deep passion burning in the heart of the Divine Masculine that they are afraid to fully embrace, because that comes with emotions. The Divine Feminine climbed on the dragon and rode it through the fire, and into the emotions. There they moved until they could see inside of this heart. It desires pure intimacy. This is Draco, and it weaves in between the two dippers, again with the yin and the yang. The dragon gives the divine counterparts the ability to embrace change, reinventing what they will allow to fill their cups. This is the first celestial encoding that we've been activated with in these channeled messages. Draco, and dragon, are both the spiritual number and soul urge number of seven which encodes the wandering to find the spiritual home. As I am working through much of the connection to these codes in the year of Seven, it seems quite fitting. Some of what I am writing is past timing, but the time resonance of fluidity means that when you read this it is in tune with your divine spacial awakening.

Last year during Jupiter and Saturn's celestial kiss, emotions were running high. This year is so much different. The emotions are deeper, and there is a swift change I feel coming in. On January 2nd we will approach 11 (2:09 AM) when Mercury enters Aquarius at 0 degrees. The Fool comes to life. This is so important to me because Gabriel holds a wand, the Magician,

Gemini, Mercury, the Divine Masculine. The wand is the key to the emotions as they create the spark of fire.

At any close junction where Mercury will be so near to Aquarius, your dreams will have been talking to you, and Gabriel says to listen. If they were already forgotten, the Draco code is within you, and you can always ask for a refresher of knowledge.

We are beginning the year fresh, and it will take the Sun fifteen days to catch us. Fifteen days, with about half of that pulling Mercury into Retrograde. Divine Masculine this tells me that you are ready to start listening to what your deep inner wishes are. You are ready to start communicating with your higher self.

I sat with this for some time. Because as we each have Divine Masculine within us, I was also aware of my calling to the awakening of my fire. I closed my eyes for guidance and was taken into the World Tree with the Jaguar and we climbed into the Heavens. Soon I arrived at a Temple for Ra, the Sun, creation. I was greeted by what I can only describe as a grey being like we have seen in UFO movies. They walked me through the sand, dragging what appeared to be a fur rug. I realized as I was moving to enter the temple, that it was my coat, and I put it on becoming Lyran. The art of Shapeshifting was noticed in myself, again.

I went into the council chamber where they started to tell me the story of this world. I was introduced to the King and the Queen, and they taught me that the Sun is the frequency of love. When we're at that frequency, there is nothing but bliss within your creation.

However, the dark matter eventually moved into their part of the universe, and it was like a storm of darkness overcoming everything. Darker and darker clouds came forward rolling across this place until there was no choice but to leave it. They left thousands of variable stars encoded with what we would need for our future. Now only several hundred RR Lyrae remain as the dark matter keeps moving and absorbing. That is why you are being given this knowledge now before it is erased.

We arrived at what I call the Purple world. It was misty, hydrogen gas. This was a purple like I have never experienced. They laid the King and Queen to rest there, and over time there was a forgetting of the Lyran bodies. The Meteorians returned to their original nodes of being, and the Lyrans followed. Eventually in this world of the purple mist, Danu, the Goddess, was born by the interracial parents, part Meteorians and part Lyran.

By this time their cultures had been deeply enmeshed, as other galactic worlds were being overtaken by dark matter, and the Sirians were soon living on this gaseous giant, as well. One such Sirians hybrid born was my long-lost Divine Masculine to Sirian and Lyran parents. I was born to a Meteorian-Lyran hybrid father with a Sirian-Lyran hybrid mother. Danu was my Godmother, of sorts. She was tasked as the teacher to guide me, but also to protect my knowledge of these days. This was not my true birth, but was a birth into the Blue Ray dimension from the Purple. Each of these worlds are portals into the dimensions where souls are record keeping and creating at growth factors we can't even begin to understand. Like molecules in the Godhead, they explain. We are exploring within the imagination of a higher level of matter.

The light eventually found its way through the mist. This dwarf star had found its way to the planet in the Draco system, with the message of death and rebirth to be encoded into the new Ophiuchus seeded beings that we were becoming. This star is what we now call WD 1856 b. It is a dead star in our current timeline, but then it was bright and gleaming with many passengers aboard. I was shown these beings as the carrier of what I have been shown before by my Spirit Guides, carriers of "salt medicine" which resides in their light bodies.

This star was broken away from the larger mass and although it was a salt giant, it was keeping a relatively low sodium diet to reduce the risk of death before achieving its mission. Stars, I am told, use high amounts of sodium and will die off before reaching the final, spectacular stages of life. We require salt, but like the stars not too much. The stars were as much alive as the beings. These light beings were the Andromedans. Interesting enough, my daughter is one of a grand generation with these symptoms of POTs and myself with Chronic Fatigue where we are currently in need if higher salt levels. I think this will balance with time. With POTs one major requirement of wellness balance is higher levels of salt. I recently read that post-Covid many people will be diagnosed with a variation of this. It is more of the molecular shift we are going through for the next life in the next world. As travelers, this could resonate with you as this world no longer feels in flow with your higher self-awareness.

They brought this message to follow the salt into the journey space. If you've read 'Celestial Spark', I talked about the channeled story where the volcano meets the ocean, and these oceans were 10% higher in salt at that time. The salt leaches out of that basaltic glass, and sparks life on terrestrial planets. You must find your balance with salt as these four ancestral teachers have guided us to. It was the salt that transformed us on this planet into our current form. But it is also awakening us. We are being activated to balance first our tau protein peptides, which are overtly activated by high sodium. The salt imbalance will deplete our memories of these activations before we can fully encode. Spirit says, "Goldilocks. Not too much and not too little,"

We must look to the Green Dragon, the Draconian Serpent, to give us the knowledge we are seeking on this journey.

Eltanin – γ Draconis (Gamma Draconis) the Zenith point, so above, you have connected to your Great Serpent guide, to loosen out of your old skin and into the new. The Zenith point is the celestial meridian. Meridians allow for the flow of energy, as is true here, too.

Each man is always in the middle of the surface of the earth and under the zenith of his own hemisphere, and over the center of the earth – Leonardo da Vinci

You are being guided to the oneness, and the unity. The unity is where the oneness becomes so still, it is in divine union with pure awareness. Duality of self is within before anything can be created outside of the salt. It preserves, enhances, develops and binds what is written in your code.

Aldibain – η Draconis (Eta Draconis), Athebyne, the Sun. This enlightenment is bright enough to guide the higher knowledge you seek. The companion of the wolf (the head of the serpent). In the saga of Eddic, Grimmismâl, the wolf will swallow the sun in the relevant stanza:

Skoll is the name of the wolf
Who follows the shining priest
Into the desolate forest,
And the other is Hati,
Hróðvitnir's son,
Who chases the bright bride of the sky.

The masculine wolf chases the Feminine energy, and the feminine wolf chases the masculine energy. The High Priest and the Priestess run until this stealth energy can run no more, and the Wolf shall swallow Eta Draconis.

It wasn't until after I received the codes that I have placed in the Chi Draconis for you, that I remembered the journey I had several nights earlier. In this journey the owl carried me to Mother Spider. Mother Spider took me to the ocean and taught me that in the water, the options were an ebb and flow that would become the morning dew on the webbing. I found that I have now become the webbing. I am integrated with my webbing.

Then I saw the serpent coming forward. It was hungry and opened up to the moon and started eating the light. As it kept eating the light, I became a serpent and started also eating the light. The light moved through my body until I was fully in my light body. In the light body I started going through a metamorphosis of bringing all of my past lives all the way back to my origins up to the surface. Shedding these lives in order to move into a brand-new space. I cannot take these past lives with me.

Then the serpent started eating the fire of the Earth and the cosmos. I followed this movement and started to eat the fire, and it began going through my body burning away the old alchemical residue and leaving the shell covered in ashes.

The serpent looked at the swords of ice and started eating them. I followed the lesson and found it cutting away all of the remaining egocentric thoughts that were keeping me from the renewal that I was seeking. In my latest transmission on the Oracle Of The Celestial YouTube Channel, I was shown that the mirror does the same. This is why you're seeking each other.

As the old thought paradigms were cut away the serpent started eating the water. As I started eating the water I flowed into the ocean and slowly sank into the depths of the oceans until I was clear. Then I fully became my light body. In my light body I rose out of the waters and into the light codes. This is what is needed to create your new beginning. This is why we are being given the code activations. This is our new beginning.

I was told in my personal code activation that everything was as promised. I felt light entering my body in what felt like geometric form, and they spread throughout my entire body. To me this was rearranging and healing my subtle body. I cried because it was so beautiful. I felt cold at first and then warm. Cold is what I usually associate with old or the past. So it was clearing out ancestral wounds.

When I moved to the solar plexus I could hear whirling, and it was like I could hear the vortexes spinning inside of me. When I asked for confirmation, I immediately heard the spinning again. When I finished, my house was set to 64° and yet I started sweating. I think I was either releasing old energy or it reset my metabolism. Since this encoding, I often feel my autonomic nervous system go into the sweating of release of old traumatic DNA. We must release it all, and it will come up until you do.

After my channeled transmission, a friend reached out to me to talk. This is one of those friends that I have known since I was in high school. She knows my woo deeply as she was the one I first astral projected with.

Everything that was coming through was deeply connected to this journey I was on, including the fact that every abstract she paints is filled with dragons. If you have read "From The Diary Of Woo" then you know after I worked with the channel of my rebirth, the dragons started coming to me. First the images were just the dragon but eventually he lost his fire and started climbing as the Mountain Goat who morphed into the Moose. I have long seen the energy of the moose as the work needed to become the Emperor. Then she came to me, the Green Maiden, who is the protector of the Green Dragon, the energy of the Divine Masculine.

These messages seemed to accelerate when Archangel Gabriel woke me up, figuratively and literally. Gabriel is associated with the white diamond fire or white light, and I also just heard associated with a white dragon. I started getting the Kundalini visions from the White Fire months ago, and Gabriel has talked about Kundalini being the Holy Spirit within us. In 2023 our new Kundalini life container has been created, so it could feel like a very transformational year for us all.

William Blake, the acclaimed poet who also happened to talk to angels, had said that the Holy Ghost is the Kundalini. Many seers and mystics through the ages have seen that Kundalini energy is Prana. Our Alta Major chakra is one of the most essential chakras as it is where so much of the implanted energy gets stuck. When this gets clogged up, the prana stops flowing. This is where Kundalini ignites, creating the Golden Ratio with the formation of energy from the Alta Major, to the Third Eye, to the Crown Chakra. The Golden Ratio runs throughout the codes.

Eta Draconis is also part of the golden triangle of three golden double stars — Athebyne (Eta Draconis), Albireo (Beta Cygni), and Almach (Gamma Andromedae). This Golden Ratio, Phi in the sky, seems to point to Almach, a quadruple star system. Pointing a direction to the four to seek the Nibiruans that fled this galaxy, before the dark matter arrives. Although I truly believe that is a diversion, which I later can confirm, I believe it was also pointing us to the center of the triangle, Alpha Cephei, known as Alderamin, which is a fast-spinning star. The Divine Feminine energy spins in the center of the Golden Ratio, creating life.

Alpha Cephei was once our North Star in 18,000 BCE. It will again be in about 5,500 years from now. I believe it spins so rapidly to hide the vortex within. In 18000 BCE during the time of the Upper Paleolithic, is when I am being shown the Tuatha Dé Danann arriving to live in the Atlantean plains that Pluto has described. If you have read 'Celestial Spark' you have read about Danu, the Green Maiden, and the arrival in the mist before. Will the portal home open in 5,500 years?

Rastaban – β Draconis (Beta Draconis), the head of the serpent, the Wolf. The download that I had was that the Draconians control the dark matter, as they were pulled through like we all were during our soul space entry. They lived in peace in the dark matter. We brought them through with us as in this dimension there is the requirement of light and darker balance.

Rastaban will eat the Sun, Eta Draconis, to hide the path forward from the Darkness. But eventually the Draconian matter will eat the Moon. The Moon I am shown as the magnetic white dwarf, GD 356, which is very unique because it shows Zeeman-split Balmer lines in pure emission. This Moon has been hiding, with the Sun's support, a terrestrial planetary companion. I have been told that the information encoded in this hidden planet must not fall into the hands of the darkness. It would block our return to the Soul Space.

Altais – δ Draconis (Delta Draconis), the Goat. Altais is able to see in darkness, and is always viewing the darkness from 320 degrees around as it moves. Any dark matter that approaches, will be drawn to Delta Draconis to be "eaten" alive. This is similar to the way that Jupiter and Saturn worked together both to create and to protect the life we needed to keep our sacred souls until the Soul Space is reopened.

Aldhibah – ζ Draconis (Zeta Draconis) is the Third Knot, or the literal Trinity Gate. This is God's Knot, or Triquetra, which holds the encoding for our birth, death, and rebirth. It holds the library of the past, present, and future. It also had the DNA to create the body, mind, and soul union, and the codes for turning stardust and gases into the terrestrial planets for each type of starseed.

Edasich – ι Draconis (Iota Draconis) is where the key to unlock the Trinity Gate resides. It is shielded behind a disc, the Pentacle of Draco. This knowledge was hidden with the Lyran codes, written in "The Gayatri", one of the oldest sacred prayers, coded in celestial formulations.

"O Thou Who givest sustenance to the universe,
From Whom all things proceed,
To Whom all things return,
Unveil to us the face of the true Spiritual Sun
Hidden by a disc of golden Light
That we may know the Truth And do our whole duty
As we journey to Thy sacred feet."

This will be awakened in all with Lyran codes as we integrate for our new Age of Aquarius. Pluto enters Aquarius on March 23 2023! We are heading into the last phase of alignment for the New Age Of Aquarius. This integration will happen after the alignment of March 23 2023 through June 11 2023, and then officially we enter the human design point of the Age of Aquarius on January 21 2024. The Age of Aquarius opens up expanded consciousness, a time when we can take control of the earth and become more mindful of the collective rights of both humans and the animals around the globe. You will feel a calling to guide others toward enlightenment, and the emotional wounds of this planet will rise to the surface.

Edasich, perhaps, hides the true Sun, so that the darkness cannot win.

Batentaban Borealis — χ Draconis (Chi Draconis), the vital energy of the serpent. This is the manifesting generator of the Serpent, Draco. The water, or Mem, 13th letter of the Hebrew alphabet, and also called 44 Draconis. Angel number 44 is being on the spiritual paths of awakening and rebirth. The Hebrew name of God is makom, with an open and a closed symbol of mem. We are both able to be open to these codes, and yet also until rebirthed will be closed off to our own sacred source.

Chi Draconis is a sacral being, and sits in the waiting position for those that seek answers. This system connects to our fourth dimension. The life force that flows through the human body that we call prana, or chi, is of the 4th dimension. Time is not the 4th dimension, I am shown. We've bent and dilated time in the 3rd dimension. So we have yet to truly see what the 4th dimension is.

Batentaban Australis — φ Draconis (Phi Draconis), the Record Keeper. This is an extremely strange, magnetic variable hydrogen star with two brighter components in the system orbiting each other. I am told this is Merkabah, the chariot, and the magnetic pull is the actual Metatron's Cube. All stars and planets have internal Merkabah, however this almost unremarkable star holds the generator of the Merkabah Craft for interdimensional travel. Batentaban Australis is numerology 2, and Metatron is associated with the number 11 which we often see listed as 11/2.

The substantial part of 2 Enoch's narrative is dedicated to Enoch"s ascent into the celestial realm. Also to Enoch's heavenly metamorphosis near the Throne of Glory. Leo, Scorpio, Aquarius and Taurus form a Cosmic Cross with Cepheus sitting on the throne. Seraph, who is the dragon, becomes.the Guardian Angel of the Oracle (Word of God). In Enoch we also read about the six-winged beings that fly around the Throne of God crying "holy, holy, holy". Draco sits at the seat of the throne now, as Draco the Serpent is the Celestial Seraphim, protecting the Trinity Gate, key, the interstellar power source and all that is encoded from the past, present and future.

Of course, the final star we are brought back to is Thuban– α Draconis (Alpha Draconis), the heart of the Universe. Standing there in the early morning hours under the tree of the universe, reminded that this star sparks the spreading of knowledge. Ophiuchus beings, your name in Latin means "Serpent Bearer". You carry and deliver the Serpent. Your brightest star is Rasalhague, which means "the head of the serpent collector".

Use your third eye to start collecting the information that this awakening has started to come in downloads.

The Draconid meteor shower will be active from 6 October to 10 October, producing its peak rate of meteors around 9 October, with the Full Moon in Pisces. These Draconian Codes are first available as a bundle with the Quandrantid Codes with the New Moon In planting them in what I call a Chi Ball on January 02 2022 - but will be fully integrated with the Full Moon in Pisces on October 09 2022. When.this information comes to you, all you must do is ask for the recoded activation to come to you from the Chi (Prana) via Batentaban Borealis for your highest good, and let the light frequency encode your higher light body. It doesn't matter what month, day or year as time is fluid.

Starseeds ... the activation is complete. When you are ready to receive this recoding, find a quiet space and relax.

Breathe deeply and allow for the light to envelop and protect you, then when ready ask Chi Draconis to send the Draconian and Quandrantid Codes activation codes.

Place your left hand out like an antenna and place your right hand in your sacral chakra. Let these codes find all of the places within that are ready, lying there for as long as you feel needed. You may see images, feel sensations, cry. There is no right or wrong as you realize the promises that are yours.

Move your right hand when ready to your solar plexus. This restarts your inner vortexes in alignment with the outer vortexes, releasing all fear, ancestral wounds, lifetime hurts. Nothing but the frequencies of love and light. You may hear spinning, or feel spinning. There is no wrong way to feel this. Stay here for as long as needed.

Then place your hands to your thighs and ask for confirmation of your activation. It may happen immediately or later in the day.

When ready, stand and let Pachamama work through the Earth Mother to rebalance your energy body. Pull the fire from within Mother Earth up through your feet, through your legs, your body, your arms, your hands, your throat, your head, releasing all energy that is not meant for you back into the cosmos to be reclaimed.

Release your connection to Chi Draconis. Wash your hands. Drink some gently salted water, eat gently what your body asks for.

This year the Sun moves into Ophiuchus on the Luna Moon phase in Pisces, In-Yô Divine, Divine Union. Luna, exactly half of our Moon will be illuminated and the other half left shadowed. This is signifying that action is ready to be taken now. This is the Year of Now. Now, is not fear. Now, is true intuitive knowing.

MURAL QUADRANT

W hen I started to prepare for creating the Chi ball for the activation codes, I was told to use not just my library of Reiki symbols, but to also incorporate Runes. Last year the most amazing man with a heart of wanderlust came into my life, Russell Penn. Russell runs the YouTube channel, Russelingaround, and is also a profound sound healer. He is in the process of developing a new Rune Tarot Deck, Liffruma, and as I am writing the book also a ninety-one card astro deck. Life, or intentionally life as a noun, the body of your cast. It is also a very masculine frequency in a creationist role. Like the version of Odin as a Seiðr, the telling and shaping of the future as gifted by Freya and his sacrifice to the well with the Tree of Life. The Life Rune deck that seems thus far to have a life of its own, shaping out some definite magic.

Last year I raked through several dozens of these runes in channeling sessions, but have not yet done anything with the astro cards. On one of my changeling sessions this rune looked at me, and so when channeling today I recognized this rune I was guided to use as Uruz, ur, the European wild ox that became extinct in 1627. Two interesting facts about this is that in Russell's deck Wild Ox is card 2, and Quadrans Muralis is no longer recognized as a constellation which makes it somewhat extinct as well. I find the symbology just sparks my delight with this path of the second code.

To me the Wild Ox card was channeled with the energy of shielding your most valued possessions, the Divine Masculine energy, passion, determination, strength. I also felt the energy of Dante step forward, who was a visionary Gemini poet that envisioned the afterlife in his most popular works. There is so much of the old masculine energy leaving this plane and the new masculine energy coming into these sessions, symbolic with this extinct ox, yet I also was shown this rune as the wandering reindeer. In the Saami tradition, this totem is like Gabriel, the White Reindeer, even believing that the tribe came from the shapeshifter, Myandash. Again, we see a synchronous energy of the shaping or reshaping frequency.

When Myandash's wife was in deep meditation, he entered her becoming one in Divine union. The Kuola Saami's believe that when she remarried, her lineage then became their people. Again and again, I am finding ancient stories of the somewhat hidden masculine energy and the sacrifice of their truth to come into the path of the inner soul.

First it was seen in the dragon codes, and here in the reindeer. The masculine is being reborn into this space where the old transactions are not going to keep them from their water center being reactivated.

As I am writing this on the evening of the New Moon, the Quandrantid showers are about ten hours out from their peak. Last night as I was channeling, I looked up at my screen and it was 10:10. We are completing cycles and making the decisions here and now to step into our guided divine purpose. When we have meteor showers, we know that they should be seen as a gift from the heavens, reminding us that we are rising out of our ashes, and this special event comes sneaking in between the dragon and the shaman. I started editing this book with the ashes of Lent, and I started my YouTube channel three years ago at the same time. It is no coincidence

Ygg, Odin in the old Norse language, is very much a part of the Christian culture of ash on the forehead as a blessing. The

Nordic pagan religion placed ashes above one's brow to ensure the protection of Odin, himself. Ash, comes after the fire.

If you remember my journey, when I started to eat the fire, it began going through my body burning away the old alchemical residue and leaving the shell covered in ashes. Now as we look at the island of Tonga covered in ash; I am being shown Ash Wednesday. Not in the terms of sinners and repentance. Instead, they are showing me that this is symbolic of the Earth realigning to its death and rebirth. Repentance in Hebrew (תשובה) meaning return. Our heart, the heart of the Mother, is beating again and reaching out to return to man.

This shower, even among meteor showers, is very special because it does not come from a comet, but rather from an asteroid. Very few astrologers put any interest into the effect an asteroid play in our chart. Cal Garrison says, "...everything is evolving, and in regularly timed cycles, other bodies are discovered—and their discovery always coincides with the birth of the principles, or "qualities" that those bodies have arrived to awaken in the collective mind." We are awakening, and it is time to look at how this coincides with the codes

Quadrans Muralis was discovered by a French astronomer called Jerome Lalande in 1795, which was a year releasing resistance including at the time of these showers when oligarchy was ended in Amsterdam. After our two years of global pandemic, I feel this is timely. There was a lot of stepping up to correct the haves and the have nots, to become more balanced in 1795. In fact, it was in this year that the story of Oak Island's Money Pit begins. That summer in 1795 a teenager named Daniel McGinnis saw strange lights on an island offshore from his parent's house, and the digging and curiosity continued ever since. That being said, then the spiritual aspect of this event comes with mystery, while seeking balance without resistance. We can't make sense of everything, and sometimes that mystery is the alchemical fire.

Why is the old masculine seeking the Holy Grail over and over again? That came to me many months later after my ascension death, and the death of Roe V Wade.

Because this encoded frequency comes from an asteroid, we are seeing parts of ourselves, stardust, information coding in the celestial cosmos. They emanate from the constellation of Boötes, the Shepard (who would be a woman) or for me the Shaman, and interestingly enough was determined just nineteen years ago to in fact be the heart, or the core of this parent comet, called C1490 Y1. This "parent" attribute was discovered in 1490 and written up in the official History of the Ming Dynasty.

The writing says that during the Ch'ing-yang event of 1490 there was a rain of innumerable stones of various sizes. The big ones were as large as a goose egg, and the small ones were the size of the fruit of an aquatic plant. Meteors explode when they are going too fast. Mercury Retrograde was not being written about until the mid-18th century, but Mercury was in retrograde during the Tunguska event in Russia that was recorded as very similar to the Ch'ing-yang event of 1490. We can hypothesize that Mercury could have also been in retrograde in 1490. We are going to see a Mercury Retrograde this January, and can expect that there will be something big that happens in our lives due to this increased speed of celestial energy. The radiant part of this shower is seen near the brightest star Arcturus at the northern tip of the constellation Boötes. I find it important to note that Boötes is herding Taurus, the Divine Bull or Divine Masculine energy.

In the German war a small area in the Netherlands was flooded by Germany and the area became a forefront of fighting for the Allied. The women and children had been evacuated before the flooding, but here in 1944, 4,000 men remained to caretake for their cattle. They would hold out here for almost five months on what became known as Man's Island, liberated weeks before the surrender of the Germans.

The Marigold plays its part in both the way the Netherlands approached this war from their hearts, but of course this flower is associated with fire and the Sun. As something that the Nazi's didn't like, seeing these flowers planted everywhere, due to its representation of resistance. Marigold is symbolic of death to the energetic control. Fire's yellow and gold chakra energies of old narratives and control are being cleared.

The Aztencians also used the Marigold herbally as a remedy for those struck by lightning (which I have written about lightning and being a Shaman), and as a benefit "for one who wishes to cross a river or water safely. This is preparing for the journey into the deep emotional heart space.

When I started the Aquarius channeled stories last year, it brought in the deep, underwater volcanos with the Warrior and the Ram. I assumed this was all Divine Masculine energy, but the truth is that the Warrior was Venus. For eight days before the Hunga Tonga-Hunga-Ha'apai volcano eruption, she went silent. She also disappeared at the end of the Mayan cycle of Venus written up in the Dresden Codex. The story started with:

"The dawn breaks and the light comes through the shadows of the misty morning dew changing the shades of colors that surround you. This is the energetic realm the collective is moving through by design of the Warrior and the Ram as we move into the timeline in which you find this story.

You welcome the soft emotions in your heart as you swim through the deep oceanic floor with the spirit of Thunnus alalunga."

Hunga Tonga–Hunga Ha'apai are twin uninhabited volcanic islands, so more of the duality of the feminine and masculine coming through our messages. In the Tongan mythology these two islands were thrown down from heaven to land on earth.

The Aquarius stories were called for the Star Beings, and they were seeking out their Atlantean world. In my latest channeled message for Week Four of the Patreon series now available on the YouTube @MindsetUnicorn channel, the Feminine is walking towards the storm, the Masculine only sees the dust storm. They are in different timelines right now.

I am reminded that Venus was once covered in water, and yet now is a hot planet covered in a cloud of dust. The Feminine and the Masculine see these seeded islands, but in two different ways. They are walking together, however, into the approaching storm. In the journey the feminine walks barefoot towards this storm, craving this storm to bring her the water she desires. Venus may yet crave water that she does not have.

On January 14th, 2022 Hunga Tonga–Hunga Haʻapai paused. As Tapukitea (Venus) returned to the storm. This eruption was the most powerful volcanic eruption that the Earth has witnessed in thirty years, with Mount Pinatubo in the Philippines being the largest eruption at the time over the last one hundred years. This eruption happened in June of 1991, just twelve years after what is a significant time of my life, and several months before I entered into an important soul contract. At the time of the Mount Pinatuba volcano, I was fully engaged in my feminine chaos of emotional imbalance. I wrote in 'Celestial Spark' that "If a hurricane meets a volcano on this journey, you could find your emotions intense." The Mount Pinatubo's eruption in the Philipines in 1991 had to deal simultaneously with Typhoon Yunya. Yunya has been said to mean beautiful girl, but in numerology it is the Number 5, our challenge for the Hierophant. An amazing wordsmith, Yunya Yang (which I love because that would be Feminine Masculine) wrote this lovely piece in Janus Literary:

"A Heart That Does Not Beat

The old woman walks on the beach barefoot. It is winter and deserted. She stays close to the water, so when the tide rolls in, it touches her skin. Years ago, she scattered her husband's ashes in the sea. Not in this sea, but all seas are connected. She is on land, however, which is unfortunate.

Chang'e flew to the moon after she became immortal. She wanted to live but didn't know the consequences of living. She has a palace on the moon. It is vast and cold. She has a rabbit. [The rabbit is the symbol of rebirth and the Empress to me.] It is also immortal and its heart does not beat. She plants a sweet olive tree.

When the old woman was a young girl, she lived on a different land, where sweet olive trees bloomed. Her husband used to bring the flowers home and arrange them in a chipped vase on the kitchen table. She no longer remembers their fragrance, but if she smells them again, she is sure she would recognize it.

Chang'e wishes there was a bridge between the moon and the earth. She wishes for a fantastic collision between time and distance. Her sweet olive tree grows. It is unattended, yet it survives."

The feminine has been walking barefoot, staying close to those churning emotions. She wishes for the bridge to be complete. It wouldn't be until February 2023 that I would realize it is the Divine Masculine that must complete the bridge.

Spirit starts singing some lyrics from Dean Lewis' song, 'Comes and Goes':

"And this part was for her and this part was for her
This part was for her, does she remember?
... It comes and goes in waves, I
Am only led to wonder why
It comes and goes in waves, I
Am only led to wonder why
Why I try"

The bridge was about to become very important to me, and also the water that led me there. It was also such a beautiful gift to find these worlds. Confirmation of the friendship blooming yet again, the remembrance of hearts, how the Empress heart does not beat until it is connected to the Emperor, and the collision that was about to happen in our world. For decades my olive tree survived, unattended, and then it was finally cared for. I wanted to live, and I did not know the consequences of coming to life. Yet I would not give up those moments of living to go back to the time before my heart was beating.

So, what about those two islands? If Yunya Yang saw these different lands, and the bridge between them, then the story of the two beginning again came to me from Lesieli Tongamohenoa, as the mythology of Tapukitea.

"It was said there were 2 fools [The Fools: a new beginning for the Divine Feminine and the Divine Masculine], Tapu from the eastern district on Tongatapu and Kitea from the western district. When Kitea heard that there was a fool in the east, she went straight on to the east to find him. When she, the female fool Kitea, arrived, he, the male fool Tapu, was hoeing his yam garden. Then she sat down at the end of his patch and yelled: «Male fool come here». He then left his hoe and came to meet the other. Then they went to the home of Tapu, and the woman was fed, and they two stayed in his place. After some time Kitea became pregnant and she said to Tapu that they should go to the west for her to conceive.

Their child was born and it was a boy, and then they decided to name it after themselves, Tapukitea. The boy grew up, but his nature was very mischievous. His parent did not get any rest of mind because of the anger of the chiefs and the people concerning the lad's conduct. They discussed then it would be better to kill their child, so that he could go and stand in the sky so that they could look up onto him, because they could not stand his behavior any longer. So was done, and Tapukitea went and stood in the sky, and since that time is his standing in the sky."

Again, the symbolism of the female Venus of other mythology and the masculine Venus of the Tongan mythology. A little too much information but yams are used by women to balance out their hormones. I love that the story says that she becomes pregnant but says they must go to the west, the Moon, the illumination, to conceive. As if they did not know until they crossed that bridge. Again, the rabbit does not have a heartbeat, and Tapukitea stands in the sky without a heartbeat. And the new high heart chakra is being recoded into the feminine and the masculine energies. We have reached the bridge. Now at the crossroads you are being given a second chance. What is it that we've created that we worry we must sacrifice? Like Odin, what knowledge will you gain?

In the Aquarius channeled story in 'Celestial Spark' more messages started to align to what we are living in now.

"Your strength lies in your voice, speak with impact through this journey and as you reunite with souls and soul fragments that you meet in this new world. Sound vibration will carry through differently in this water world than it does in the Middle and Upper realms. Like the energy of the upcoming Mercury Retrograde, the sounds you create now will travel with a speed beyond your capacity to understand in the current time we reside in. At the top of the oceanic realm, it travels at five times the speed of sound in the world above. However, you are swimming deep, at 1,300 feet below the surface and the intensity of sound is not only faster but comes at you more densely. You are projecting peace, and will stay calm in times of adversity and as you hatch ideas in this deeply hidden realm, they will leave your body and hatch quickly."

As the volcano blasted itself out of the ocean a shockwave was produced as a sonic boom, close to the speed of sound. The sonic boom was heard as far away as New Zealand more than 1,300 miles away, and Alaska more than 6,000 miles away. Eventually this shockwave traveled halfway around the world— as far as the United Kingdom, which is located a staggering 10,000 miles away.

On the evening of January 13 2020 just before this explosion, the Winter Circle which is an asterism composed of the brightest stars in the constellations of Canis Major, Orion, Taurus, Auriga, Gemini, and Canis Minor stood upright in the sky with The Milky Way passing vertically through it. Aldebaran being one of these specific stars in the Winter Circle. Come Spring when the two events with Arcturus, the Spring Triangle and the Virgo Diamond, will occur. I am being told that Arcturus is currently moving from the lower chakra colors into its light body. This timing of course does not have an awareness of our life patterns, but it is similar to what we are seeing in this recode. It is currently soft orange, sacral energy moving into the solar plexus. This could be why it is so important to move the Draconian Codes into our system with the combined codes of the Quandrantid Codes now as we move through the portal of the Winter Circle.

There was a seed planted in March of 2021 when the New Moon moved through a portal located between Aldebaran and Mars. The moon was 33 percent illuminated. The top of Hunga-Tonga-Hunga-Ha'apai peaks just 330 feet above sea level. Synchronous messages are always coming towards us.

The New Moon on January 2nd 2022 just before this all started, was at 10:33 PST. Spirit is saying this was the completion of that seed being opened to start our growth cycle now. We are nearing the Spring Equinox, when our seeds will start to sprout into the third dimension from the intention below, to grow into our daily lives over the next year. Many of us that followed the 2021 initiations knew this was our path forward. We followed the fire. I talk at length about the fire in my "From The Diary Of Woo' book. This January New Moon in 2021 was of course the 19th, the tarot number for the Sun, which is symbolic of birth. Today when I met the fire, the Nastas Priestess came with me. I sat around the fire, pulling out old shadow cords that had served my karma, but were no longer mine. She took the fire like a sparkler on the Fourth Of July and waved it around in the air. When she looked into my eyes it was as if she threw down the fire in a magical meteor of explosion, and the fire erupted all around us. It was the fire of protection, love and being loved. Earlier in the day, speaking of the Moon, the Jaguar has surrounded my journey, and as the shadows started to cage me, Jaguar rebutted and pushed out the windows of the cage. Boldly stated, I was not to be caged, but as well, you was in a protective space.

As I had opened up to this journey, I started digging into my heart. I was covered in tar, and my heart was black. Slowly the more I dug, the more opened, and soon I was carved open from navel to forehead and the channel was being wiped clean by myself. I felt the drip of water, and as the waters ran down from the Heaven's into my deep wounds, a snake appeared and transformed into an eel. Eel then began rubbing its skin down the sides, spaces were being cleared and soon the entire area was clean. I was given balm that I rubbed into the wounds, and was given robes that were made like bandages to wrap around my being, and I sat around the fire and started to feel the lifetimes of love that I had forgotten, or that maybe had forgotten me.

This was shown to me because I could not understand why these codes were about realigning the chakras. We started far below the earth, the initial codes of the celestial kingdom. It comes up through the fire, and the water, and there we start again to awaken to a knowledge that is greater than ourselves. These are not just planetary or celestial codes; these are the codes of us. They are what was created to become us, and what will be left behind after us. The fire is never to be put out again, and so we cannot stop our hearts from awakening. The love that was ours, cannot ever be erased. The shadows that we are done with, do not stop the lessons on our path forward, but they do mean that maybe we are meant to move forward no matter where our partner may be. That story, of love, waits for another day.

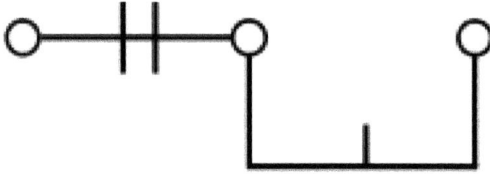

TIÀNQUIZTLI

W hen I started to talk to the Pleiades, they said that before we could move into the Water Codes, we had to work through the Fire Codes. As I had been working with the Nustas Priestess, I didn't know that she would come back almost a year later and bring me the Initiations of the Nusta Karpay, which is the sacred healing rites with Pleiadian star transmissions. The codes that I was being given are more ancient, as they are aligned to our Blue Ray fire body, and this aligns the three; Crown chakra, Third Eye chakra,

Alta Major chakra. We are awakening what I call the Godhead within our being, through and alignment in our Solar Plexus chakra. The Pleiades is the code that moves from the Heart chakra, through the divine union in the High Heart chakra, into the Throat Chakra, and then it brings in new beginnings in the Alta Major chakra, tapping into the Third Eye chakra. The Pleiades holds on to a new beginning within it, but it is energized by the fire of the divine counterparts through that High Heart chakra. This is where the Ophiuchus, our Blue Ray energies come from the heart of our beings, and channels into our life container. It is only after we have fully activated, that we can fully connect to the Andean healing path.

I find it interesting that the High Heart chakra started coming out in the readings in Capricorn first. I have always seen Capricorn as "little deaths" as a very transformational energy. However, in Kabbalah tradition Capricorn is associated with Yod. Yod is connected to that sacred energy of iodine. Iodization is the process of fortifying salt for humans, and salt is very sacred for me. It purifies and cleanses, and it clears negative energy from our energy field. Ionization is in celestial work when one (or more) electron is stripped off or added to the atom, it is no longer electrically neutral and an ion is formed. This is when the atom is said to be ionized. I am sure more about what this means will come in as the channel opens, but what is meant to be known right now is that the coordination number of Iodine is 3, which is pyramidal and 44 pm (particulate matter). It has a coordination number of 6, with

95 pm. As well, its ion charge is a plus 7. My jaw dropped as I read this in the edits thinking all about being now in the year of seven, 2023.

Seven is what I have called The Year of Karma, but I was being shown it as Water, our gift. Our work to our sacred cells will have to go through the 777. Work is made to be done, so it is and so it will be. I am being shown that 07-07-2023 and 08-08-2024 will be two of the most important portals of our lifetime.

The Pleiades align one side of this portal protection from 444 light years away from Taurus. Aldebaran is the Bull's eye - watching over with great care. In the Winter Circle Aldebaran is in Taurus. After our "birthing season", which was confirmed by Tapukitea, these codes of the Pleiades will shine from dusk until dawn. The Seven Sisters, our main seven chakras being the light language of the masculine energy of Taurus. Angel number 444 is just another sign of the collective forced spiritual awakening.

Our soul lives in the multiverse. Our soul is an ocean and our reality is a drop of that ocean where we are both the ocean and yet separate from the ocean. But the week I wrote this we all saw that the ocean is not separate at all as it moved across the planet.

In most lifetimes we come here to work with soul contracts to learn valuable lessons to heal the collective oceans and raise the frequency of both what we will call Heaven and Earth. Heaven being what most people see as the New Earth, which is already created. The realism of what the New Earth is, is not going to be created for a lot of our reality years, but our reality is mere seconds of the spiritual realm. What we have been through over the last few years was the healing of these planes.

If Zen is the art of seeing into the nature of one's own being, which points the way from bondage to freedom - then if we do not work on our inner healing we are bound to the old hearts of the feminine and masculine. This is the unconscious heart. Some of us have chosen to stay unconscious to activate what is needed later, and the others of us are activating now as teachers. I started working on these aspects in my client program to embody these new energies in the yin-yang of our beings, and will continue until complete.

While we can come into a relationship with our divine partners without doing the work at the highest level, what many teachers are teaching is more from the Divine Feminine wound and illusion of control. I, too, trusted that old power of the feminine wounded heart. It was meant to be what tool me from dream to reality. The drop to reality was hard.

Eventually even in the greatest of relationships when there isn't healing growth of the frequency, and healing of the wounds, they will turn toxic. Partners, friends, family, lovers, all things turn toxic when they sit in stagnation for too long. This they have called "energy fermentation".

The New Moon, again as an end of the germination cycle of our Spiritual Seed, brought with it the Comet Leonard to shine one last bright message before leaving our galaxy being shot out of it by the Sun. I was told in November that the wind was coming for the Divine Masculine. I shared a photo of solar winds detaching the Divine Masculine from Comet Leonard on January 4th the morning after 2022's first New Moon. NASA noted that Leonard made a 40,000-year journey to our sun from the outer solar system, but the comet was only discovered on January 3rd, 2021 – just one year before the perihelion, when it gets to its closest distance to the Sun to be sent on its next mission. Angel Number 4, a significance of the angel number 4 indicates that you are getting the love and assistance of your guardian angels. Number 4, the Emperor. This New Moon on March 21 2023 is in Aries, The Emperor, and the First House of new beginnings. This is the day after we mark our Spring Equinox, which is a Wicca rite of Ostara, one of three festivals on the Wheel of The Year. The Earth is becoming the Maiden, awakening her buds as she starts to bloom. In Tarot, this is the Empress energy. We are awakening Union.

Do you remember me talking about the winds and the Divine Masculine in the channeled message on 11/07? I also believe the winds are carrying the ash of the volcano to lower the fast-rising temperatures on this planet, and that is healing. A sign of protection for any that take up this journey. This year the wheat fields desire a waterfall, and so I have channeled about the level of water (which they called torrential rains) that we've been having. This is the storm that brings life, and she is complete.

There are actually thirteen Comet Leonards out there, and I know with Ophiuchus and Bluerays coming into our world as the thirteenth zodiac last year, this is just confirmation it was time. The Empress in Tarot wears a crown of 12 stars, and of course she is the 13th, that is the channel of creation within us all. Ophiuchus is technically the ninth zodiac position, but for myself it will always be that thirteenth tribe. Aries may be the traditional First House, but Sagittarius is not only rebirth but that's expansive energy from Jupiter that needs to be in place to work with Saturn to create life. Just Google "Jupiter is a vacuum + Saturn" to learn about this amazing celestial birth aspect. We are off our axis, but all is coming in as we've asked it to.

Unexpectedly to many of us, this thirteenth comet was close enough for it to potentially be seen from your own backyard. This was too a meaning to help energetically awaken the collective out of our slumber before the rumbles started. We had several days of energetic messages and then Venus moved away into her eight days of renewal. The eighth day is about rebirth. Scorpio saying, "Now we go to sleep so that creation can take place." This week of my editing Jupiter and Venus are once again in the sky watching and planning. We're heading into something beautifully expanding.

The origin of Comet Leonard is likely from a distant sphere of comets called the Oort Cloud, which is a vast reservoir of millions, or perhaps billions, of comets.

They showed me the destination of Nibiru, Planet X. Recently an item called TG387 and nicknamed "The Goblin" — was spotted by astronomers at the Carnegie Institution of Science using a giant Japanese observatory in Hawaii called Subaru. The Carnegie team first spotted the object in 2015 and then followed it on its journey around the Sun for the last four years. Those observations revealed an incredibly distant target. TG387 takes a whopping 40,000 years to complete just one orbit around the Sun. Do you see the synchronous alignment there? I wrote about this planet for the Mystic Lights in the book, 'Celestial Spark'.

"Nibiru, the planet known to the ancient Babylonians. This was seen in ancient Sumerian writings, and is associated with the celestial body, the god Marduk, "bull calf of the sun". I am reminded of Kusarikku ("Bull-Man"), who has the Ur(i)dimmu ("Dog-Man" or "Lion-Man") walking with him. So many signs of the old masculine energy and the masculine energy being so bound to each other. And the masculine walks this part of the journey alone, male or female we all have this energy of action within us that the feminine side of our nurturing is birthing anew. I have let all of the masculine energies around me, and within me, go. Freedom is what was asked for, and the Jaguar watches the feminine heal. The Priestess today showed me that she was purging out the toxins they are cleansing from our hearts, and that means you too must spit out the last bits of that energy, old heart energy of green goop, so you can walk into the indigo space of the unknown future. Once I did this myself, I saw myself in the field of the Goddess, fully pregnant, with the sun and joy beaming all around myself.

There was no masculine yet, the bull calf, the new masculine was being born in the past memories I was gifted to view. Masculine, very soon, you are fully born. Sagittarius is my sign of Mystic Lights but can resonate with those twin flames, mirror souls or when feeling aligned to angel numbers, the Nimurians or dragon medicine. You may be drawn to recode your genetic body through light language. Ophiuchus is also deeply attached to Sagittarius for rebirth.

This last week I saw a comic egg filled with dragons, and a two-headed dragon that is attached to the next level of channeled messages. The Dragon Medicine had to come breath its fire into our encoding so that we would start this beautiful adventure to the edge of our existence. Two weeks later they found a "little dragon" on an uninhabited Australian island and proclaimed it as a new species.

I had also recorded a video and scheduled it for the day after Comet Leonard was discovered - that was January 04 2021. In the video on YouTube I talk about the Sun burning away their armor. This week, just over two years later, another YouTube divination channeler posted a video about the "Sun Alchemizing The Earth and All Who Reside". I haven't watched that video but the title was another sign to me that what I had channeled was true. Just chills over all of the synchronous energy here!! Burning is heat, and heat creates fast change. His is that energy the collective needed in those two warm chakra centers as we start to create something very special through the "energy fermentation". Once we hit that emergence, I was told we will cool down a lot, which is part of the Golden Transmissions I started to tune into after writing these sessions down. We are now into the cold fermentation.

The archaic energy of the fermentation process is the body frequency of either agitation or excitement. The gut being chemically sparked by the energy of stagnation. When stuck it sits in frustration. These first two codes were to awaken us out of the stagnation. I talked about this on my podcast. Fermentation and germination are disruptors in the plants and in our bodies.

Fermenting these chemicals breakdown our inner and outer subtle body using substances of bacteria, yeasts, or other microorganisms, or microenergies typically involving effervescence. Spirit and effervescence are semantically related in characteristic topics. In some cases, you can use "Spirit" instead of the noun "Effervescence", when it comes to topics like life, or animation. Collective effervescence (CE) is a sociological concept coined by Émile Durkheim. A community or society may at times come together and simultaneously communicate the same thought and participate in the same action. Such an event then causes collective effervescence which excites individuals and serves to unify the group. The tragedies of 9/11 did this in some ways, the horrific fires in Australia as well. But the pandemic is the global collective working on a forced awakening.

Fermentation gives off heat. If we think in terms of inflammation, we apply heat for muscle pain or stiffness. When we become too rigid, heat is applied.

So how do we get out of the heat and into the excitement frequency to click open in a more aligned, and less caustic state? We have to introduce the cold. When fermenting at cold temperatures, yeasts produce carbon dioxide and other molecules more slowly and steadily. Cold in my body was a sensation that was happening when my body would do a massive cellular dump. My cells were hiding large amounts of histamine and when opened I would feel that physical coldness.

When I started doing energetic work, I felt cold when working on deep ancestral or astral energies or very warm when working on something that requires speedy delivery. When we work alone the process is only a minuscule leap ahead for the collective. Since we collectively are generally not working in unison, we change but those around us may not.

When we work at the collective effervescence level it is reminiscent of the sacred circle of the clan. When the entire tribe gathers together becoming a sacred event, a high energy level comes into play. This energy can get directed onto physical objects or people which also become sacred. This is why the totems were created. As a symbol of the clan this Huaca, which I talk about in my book 'From The Diary Of Woo' can be called in times of need for anything from protection to insight.

This weekend when I went into a sacred space with my global clan, in my first journey I was very much in the mist. I went into this misty forest and into my eye, and the eyes came back into today's circle. The ancient initiations we were talking about include weaving energetic clothes covered in symbolic eyes. The cords of the shadow that I removed and released back to where they came from to continue their work elsewhere, were connected to the eyes, the optical and the limbic system. In the mist, when these codes were coming in, in my mind's eye, Mother Spider asked me what I was willing to see. We had been talking about this idea of remaining nimble, which I am shown is both about being in our light energetically, but also being agile to adapt in body and mind.

As I walked down this dark path Mother Spider swung in front of me guiding my path to where I was taken to a boat. As the mist dissipated, I was on the water in Venice in a boat but could not see what was behind me. I went under several bridges before the journey came to the end with the message that I am always connected to my soul.

Thomas Kinkade is my Upper Realm Teacher and Guide. He has many masterpieces that are paintings of this part of Venice that I traveled through. He told me on a later journey that when I see the mist, he is calling me to lessons. Kinkade was called the "Painter of Light". He passed just before we entered this new b'ak'tun in the Mayan new calendar in 2012. His art is spiritual Huacas hanging in homes across the world that can be used to tap into this sacred space. "It's not the world we live in," Kinkade said of his painting, "it's the world we wished we live in. People wish they could find that stream, that cabin in the woods."

Like myself, Kinkade was an alcoholic that found sanctuary in this work with his spiritual gift. However, I believe that he literally died in his dark night of the ego, having been awakened by his girlfriend at the time. I don't know if she was more than a karmic soulmate, she very likely could have been a divine partner. I like to think this Spiritual part of him is working with me (and probably many others) to save me from hitting the deep lows that took his life. His gallery has stated that, "If there was ever a place to fall in love, it would be here. Any visitor arriving in Venice is immediately transported into another world." And I understand then why he took me there. Transporting me in the water is very reminiscent of the Soul Space I have written about.

As we went around the sacred circle sharing our adventures, I found that each person had a collective message I was told to "see" by Mother Spider. We have been through such a long several years of separation, which could feel very internally separate for your inner being. Some of you through this global spiritual essence or forced awakening are feeling the loneliness of going through your darkness alone. Let this be your mist that lets you know you are not alone. The light is always there. 2022 is the Year of The Tiger starting on February 1st. We must work with Tiger singularly, before the Empress arrives in massive numbers.

In the circle the masculine tiger came out first talking to my feminine tiger saying that our hearts beat together. Remember that what the masculine is saying right now can be falling on the deaf ears of the feminine in her movement through this storm. What is important to note is that our inner and outer energies are meant to be supportive of each other rather than creating guilt and grief for following our path of light. The tiger took us to the bridges that I was under. The bridge to each other is still being built. It is not yet completed. Weeks ago, I was shown that the Masculine has to complete the bridge. It is their work, and Feminine cannot force it. I see this metaphorically and very aligned to the fact that we are still in the soup of this global disease. We need a little courage, take and go within the tiger to gain courage and strength in this new year. Some people may see a tiger and others a jaguar. They come from the same galactic and feline family.

Then the other sacred travelers joined the circle. The Lioness, the Empress, gave of her heart. This is why her heart is not beating in the Moon palace.

The Serpent came in to give us the energy to clear fear.

The Hawk came in to bring us the Stardust to remind us that we are not just made of stardust, but are all connected through the stardust.

These guides ask us to stay in this space for a moment open to receive these gifts. Even with the chaos that can be around us and swirl and swim in our thoughts, we are safe to open our hearts and our minds.

Then the Swan, who I see as the Divine Feminine energy, the mate of the masculine Tiger, Amor, came in to again remind us to be agile and not so rigid.

She became Mother Bear, the protector of the North closing the cross of the circle. These sacred star circles are so important to our journey, through our birthing cycle.

The symbol of the cross has come into our journey many times already in this channeled book. February 8th, 2020, just four days before I opened my YouTube channel, there was a Cross and a number 7 filled in the sky above Israel. Mother

Spider is weaving this into my head, there is something meaningful about incorporating mudras into our journey to connect to your ancestors. In the past using our fingers to create mudras representing the five elements was very important, and if we add in Pachamama and the Æther, we have seven elements.

The cross has become such a symbolic messenger for me. Recently in a sacred initiation of the gnostic and kabbalistic practice of Sophia, I saw the Southern Cross anointing this sacred yurt we were in. This beautiful group of Feminine Warriors chanting, and dancing, and calling in our divine union within. This channeled cross then took me to Pisces and the Turtle medicine. I was being guided to the new masculine energy that had passed at age four, protecting all of the feminine energy that passed through the sacred veil of this temple.

Our ancestors are always there to keep us safe. On the other side they are as ancient as we, and we often struggle to break away from the mentality of time constructs. However, I am being asked to note, Mother Bear was wounded. The caregiver of the temple was also wounded by a great loss.

The myth from the California Sierra and Paiute tribes says that "One day Grizzly mother ate Deer mother. Deer sisters retaliated by trapping Grizzly sisters in a cave." This may have been the storm that Mother Bear was warning us about. We are moving into the "school of learning" having been purified of energetic blocks to the subtle body.

This is a reminder that we must keep unwinding those karmic lessons as we are only in the alchemy of our current auric body. Clearing space for the next level of our soul's journey.

I am not religious, barely attended church when I was a toddler, but in 1 Corinthians 14:1-40 ESV / it says:

"Pursue love, and earnestly desire the spiritual gifts, especially that you may prophesy. For one who speaks in a tongue speaks not to men but to God; for no one understands him, but he utters mysteries in the Spirit. On the other hand, the one who prophesies speaks to people for their upbuilding and encouragement and consolation. The one who speaks in a tongue builds up himself, but the one who prophesies builds up the church."

I see this as the clan. When we gather on these practices, on YouTube, or in the Sacred Space, we are all speaking to the prophecy that is meant for our collective ascension. There are those that are going to tell you just enough to make you a slave to the "church of them". This has nothing to do with making money or popularity because money is an energy exchange. Spirit does require that we give and receive. Find those that see you as a partner in the collective creation, but not those that see you as a resource for their desires.

This brings me back to that message where our partners, friends, family, lovers, all things can turn toxic when they sit in stagnation for too long. Anything that is not moving that fermentation along can turn sour and create a cloud rather than a mist. Remember that as we continue.

When you are fermenting foods one of the most common visible contaminations is a white, cloudy substance called Kahm yeast. While Kahm yeast isn't harmful it can indicate that there is a problem with your ferment. In vinegar pickles, a cloudy brine is more concerning and may indicate spoilage or contamination. Vinegar as a preservative can be holding you in place. However, in a fermented brine the cloudy brine is a clue that you are creating that healthy bacterial community. Even beer can become cloudy or hazy, but the secret is in the cold stable haze. Cold comes from that inner, deeper work.

When I continued my journey with the group, the path was sunny. I was walking barefoot, always barefoot lately, and the path turned into sand. I walked onto the beach and danced. Remember that each grain of sand has its place, and yet because of the ocean and the elements sand is always changing or exchanging energies.

I saw a starfish that appeared to be dying. Starfish are my symbol of our wishes. I can believe that we all have a dying wish or two within us right now. As I picked up the starfish, I could feel its past trauma and the abuse it had suffered. Bullying was a big part of what I felt. I saw that it had been thrown far away from where it knew it belonged. I felt that sadness.

I walked with the starfish in my hand into the ocean until it told me it was far enough out. I looked back to the beach and it was far far away by now. Instead of getting afraid, I turned onto my back and became a starfish, floating in this blissful energy of the ocean letting myself be in the flow state.

As I was floating, I fell asleep and Eagle picked me up and took me to the upper realm. Thomas Kinkade greeted me and we walked into the studio. At the edge of the clouds and the edge of the beach I could see the sun on the horizon. He said, "The difference between the Sunrise and the Sunset is just a little different shading of perspective. He taught me to paint the two and then we walked through the Upper Realm deep in conversation.

I was told last night the next code comes from the Stars Storm in the Pleiades. It literally is a dust cloud or called an open star cluster that were all born around the same time from a gigantic cloud of gas and dust. The brightest stars in the formation glow a hot blue and formed within the last 100 million years. Blue is both symbolic of the hottest hot and the cold. Communication is important to our storytelling to glean deeper messages in the codes. And now we see that the Divine Masculine sees the storm, and so who is really seeing the true timeline?

Luca Parmitano, an ESA astronaut currently resident on the International Space Station as a member of the Expedition 36 crew, posted a photo and wrote: "The Mediterranean, the Pleiades and a storm in the distance." The storm is coming, the storm is here.

This year has been the year of the "particulate" matter, wearing masks that are meant to filter out the viral particles. If the Fire is our third energy (technically the fourth if we consider the portal 0 as the first) and Water our fourth energy, we are moving from the space of walking through our emotions into our true strength. We are being guided that we must start waking up to what we are doing to our air quality on this planet. We are oxygen requiring creatures and yet one of the top ten causes of death currently is directly the pollutants in our air. If you look into this on the NASA website, they say that "studies show people who breathe more PM are more likely to develop lung cancer, lower respiratory infections, chronic obstructive pulmonary disease (COPD), and problems during pregnancy and birth, such as preterm birth and low birth weight." It is important that we remember we are one. We each have hundreds of billions of atoms that were once in everyone else's bodies, but we have approximately 1 atom in our body from every breath that every human has ever taken.

Part of what came through in the Fire session was the energy of our red blood cells, which if you have followed me for at least six years on social media, you know that it takes about four months for our bodies to regenerate all new red blood cells. Our blood cells and our bacterial cells that live in and on our body make up most, ninety-six percent, of what we call the body. In truth only four percent of your body is bones, muscles, organs, and the skin that we use as coverage, or identity. These bacterial cells are the aliens that I talk about in my wellness practice a lot. There are a million of these cells per square inch of your skin. What you see in the mirror, is not you. It is a projection of the alien contribution to what you call, 'you'.

Separation ... That is what the mirroring eventually leads to for most divine partners. It isn't the end, but it is the source of why we are meant to meet. We meet to activate something, a yearning and calling to our soul purpose. Then we often walk separate paths. Yet, it still makes you feel emotionally drained.

The deeper feelings that you have for them, especially if you haven't spoken your truth, has come for many reasons. Some of it can be because you are learning things about how you work with others based on the experiences you have had in life. Communication is all about responses. If you stop responding in truth - you are not in communication as much as they aren't. There is a two-party system that creates ghosting energy. Communication is a loop of interactions with others. And this loop is very personal - for you both. We filter our communication based on our own perceptions of the world. These come from what we have experienced, and then we seek the loop by looking in the mirror.

The mirror is going to show you mostly non-verbal energy. We communicate 93% of our meaning through non-verbal communication. This includes body language, voice inflection, postures, gestures, expressions. Only 7% of the communication comes from the actual words used. So, when you are reading this book, or communicating with someone via text, chat, server, email, there are missing parts of the loop even deeper than you realize. When we truly communicate at the cellular level, that is something exceptional.

Here is what I have learned in my own mirror soul experiences, since in the current state of being most of your communications are only that 7% of words. First, always ask the other person what they need from you. Repeat communication back to them to make sure you understand. See their side of things, and approach the situation with a positive intention. Close the loop by being specific, knowing what you want and asking for that. Make sure they understand what you want, and offer options. No one does well with only one choice - as that is an ultimatum. Ask yourself, what response am I looking for? What result am I seeking?

Realize that you can't ask for too much in the messages. We have a safety valve on our senses and after you have asked about half a dozen things of someone, they will be overloaded with sensory issues. When you are in person it may feel like a daze because the senses are already overloaded with the energetic sensory connection. You are each seeking the other 93%. Be flexible in letting the situation build itself out from the life filter that each of you bring to the space. Their unique experiences will help you grow as will yours. We often attract someone with different culture, age, beliefs, values, interests because we have asked to shift our own experience in this lifetime.

How will you know when you've reached the "union point" or max point or the "zenith" of understanding with the other soul? Think about how it will feel, what you will hear, and how it will appear to you. Does it achieve what you wanted with the response and results you were seeking? If not, this soul is only meant to teach you, and move on. However, sometimes they are meant for something more. Most of this will come in without any actual communication until you reach that last seven percent. We must work through the heavy work of our beings, the mass of our beings, before we are ready to use our own sound waves. Mother Earth says it is time.

Most of our body mass is oxygen, which is why breathing is so important. Hydrogen and carbon make up the most of the other largest percent of your body composition, and everything else makes up about seven percent of the atomic body. We are working from the magma up, through the core of the earth, into our bare feet, up through the fire center, into the water center, and then we will activate air.

Did you know that you have more atoms in your body than the entire universe has stars? This is why I think it was so poignant that Hank Wesselman in my journey last year told me that we are rainbows made of stardust. Light bodies, light frequencies made of stardust. The rest just isn't you. It only contributes to your human experience. You are a soul, a light being. This body is atomic and mass is unmeasurable in many of the ways we judge that being.

The greatest number of atoms in our bodies are oxygen and hydrogen, and that comes directly from drinking enough water and breathing enough air. Our hydrogen atoms are contained in the atmosphere, and the water on the earth. But we must focus on the air before we return to the gift of the water.

Ethan Siegal on Forbes wrote: "If you were to take all of the atoms in your body and let them return to the natural environment of the Earth, and you then thoroughly mixed all the air and water on the Earth, you'd realize a couple of spectacular facts.

One out of every 21 quadrillion hydrogen atoms (2.1×10^{16} atoms) come from your body.
One out of every 26 quadrillion oxygen atoms (2.6×10^{16} atoms) come from your body.

And this is true for everyone's body, on average, when you consider the atoms that made them up a year ago." Everything that surrounds you, has some spark in it from your body. You are deeply connected into this matrix, this grid of life.

You are made up from the atoms of everything that has ever been on this planet. How does it feel to be a live T-Rex? Every atom within our Earth biosphere has resided within us all, living or dead. Atomically you are both the past and the future, and everything that ever made up this planet, within this system, within this dimension. We are it.

Just before the new ba'ka'tun, Mayan calendar, started in 2012 researchers found the twin planet of Earth. This planet comes from the source of the initial creator, Pachamama. This is our cosmic twin that they call now Kebler-78b. The binary other us, and it comes in with the number of both shadow work, and divine union. Kebler-78b is, of course, 400 light years away. The four is shadowing this session. Kebler-78b was found in the constellation Cygnus, the Swan. Scientists do not know how this twin planet was created. When they have put it into their known data models for planetary creation, nothing matches where it is, or how it acts. It is also a fire planet, made mostly of iron and rock like Earth, but covered by molten lava rock on the outside, like a protective shield. I feel that this has been covered because we were not ready for the fire that lies within this planet, and so the Fire Codes lie within this Space.

They opened the portal with the underwater volcano, and now we just need to align to those codes.

Both New Zealand and Tonga belong to the Polynesian Triangle. The native Māori people of New Zealand share genetic and cultural similarities with the people of Tonga. In New Zealand they found the bones of an extinct swan at Te Whanga, a lagoon off the east coast of New Zealand. So, this is a very ancient and sacred code we are reactivating. The fire comes from the warriors and sacred healers within us all. The extinct feminine and masculine hearts are ceremonially being laid to rest, as we move into higher consciousness.

Cygnus is known also as the Northern Cross. I am brought back to the cross and the number 7 that showed up in the sky, and the Axis Mundi cross where the Heavens meet the Earth. The center being Thurban, our ancient pole star, Sadr is the pole star for Mars who shows me that he rules Aries, our fiery Emperor of the tarot. Sadr is the center of the Southern Cross. If the center of our Northern Cross is where we find our North Node, our soul's purpose in this life, then perhaps the Southern Cross is where we find our South Node, where we work through what needs to be shed in order to grow and ascend with the energy of the Serpent. We talk a lot about nodes, but they are our heart connections to above and below.

The Swan brings so much significance into my world after the channeling of the 'Celestial Spark' stories, and the divine lovers. One of the stories of the Swan constellation is that of the race between Cycnus and Phaeton. Phaeton is the mortal son of Helios, the God of the Sun. Cycnus is just another spelling of the word, Cygnus, meaning the Swan in the Greek language. The Greek God Ares (Aries) is the ruler of Mars. Most people do not see that there is a connection between the Aries Ram and the Ares to God who is often shown as the Wolf. However, the Ram to me is a divine masculine symbol, as is often the Wolf. The Ram is the Wolf in disguise, as we have been told in our fairy tales. I am just now being told that the Divine Masculine will come into the third codes like a Lion, roaring in their third dimensional Emperor's codes; and move out like a newborn lamb. This is their new heart, and they may play in the disguise of the Wolf until they are ready to show their truth. In 2023 March came in like a Lamb and will go out like a Lion, so it may not be that the new masculine is going to come into their full embodiment in 2023. We are all still in a metamorphosis of something. The eel turns into the fish, and the fish when they come into divinity create that Piscean Twelfth House of endings, or evolution. As we enter Aries season in 2023, perhaps the Divine Masculine energy is in my card 22, In-Between.

Back in the story, Cycnus is the son of Ares, is best friends with Phaeton. When they steal the chariots and race into the sky, they come too close to the fire of the Sun and are sent back to Earth where Phaeton falls into the river and dies. Cycnus goes to Zeus to ask for help, and says he will sacrifice himself by only living as long as a swan's life if Zeus will help him get his friend to give him a proper burial. I am shown this as being the masculine sacrifice that must happen to truly create from their new heart, their higher heart that has been awakened. If Phaeton would have had the ability to breathe underwater, he would have lived. How do we learn to breathe through our emotions?

As well in Chinese mythology there is a similar story. February 1 2022 marks the Year of the Tiger, another of my symbols for the divine lovers. Of course, how poetic that 2023 will be the Year of The Water Rabbit, the emotional Empress. In this story they tell us of the Magpie Bridge. The Milky Way is seen as the auroral arc, or rainbow bridge of the Axis Mundi. In this story Niu Lang is an immortal fairy, and Zhi Nu a mortal. They fall in love and the Goddess of Heaven forbids it. If we think of the channeled messages of "Celestial Spark' with the Goddess Danu being the protector of the divine lovers, it would make sense that she would deny this union before it was divine timing. The Magpies are a part of the Crow and Raven family, which brings in ancient knowledge, an understanding of the rebirth process. These magpies in this story build a bridge so that each year during the Southern Cross the lovers may unite. There is going to be a big collective change with these Sun codes that are coming. I feel a big shift in the collective in June 2022. June 1, 2022 is the date I give as my personal Scorpionic death. This was the death of my old heart. I am now shifted into a different timeline, or perhaps merged timelines. I have completed my Earth School and the rest of this life is mine before I move to the Fifth Dimension. I will not return to another life on Earth School.

Then it hits me, the auroal arc, the rainbow bridge. The masculine energy has entered the mountain, they're inside of the cave. They see the storm, and that storm is the borealis, and that rainbow will bring them to completion. But they first set the fire in the cave, and what they see on the cave walls is perception and nothing more. They have to see things through their own eyes, before they can see through their heart.

The shift in our new hearts starts with fire, the tetrahedron which perpetuates balance and stability. Our next session will move into the icosahedron which is associated with water to enhance our creative thought and expressive manifestation generator. Last session will move into the dodecahedron to connect into the universe to our higher self through the ancient mystic mystery of "you". To me this has already started. I was drawn to start training in trauma release yoga this year, and the first lesson was that "The Beginning of Yoga (you) is Now." This shift is the Golden Ratio, which is finally coming into the transmissions. This is representing perfect harmony, or the most attractive proportion in almost all things. We are aligning into our perfect harmony of frequency, light and sound bodies.

I am reminded that Eta Draconis is a part of the golden triangle of three golden double stars — Athebyne (Eta Draconis), Albireo (Beta Cygni), and Almach (Gamma

Andromedae). Albireo is the head, the ancient knowledge of the Swan. We had to move through the swan to gain the knowledge we had forgotten. Some of this knowledge came in with the 'Celestial Spark' stories, and Goddess Danu, the Protective Mother. In the Libra channeled stories for the White Fire Tigers, we were first introduced to the Moon Goddess as The White Tiger, but she has now shown herself as Chang'e. Her partner is the Green Dragon, who drinks the drug of immortality to be the protector of the Cosmos forever more. He is known as the Emperor, called Lord Archer, Hou Yi who is the Slayer of Suns.

Hou Yi saw ten suns in the sky, the other nine planets and the Sun is what I believe them to be. Hou Yi came to this planet to rein in the suns so that the Earth would not become a fire planet. Slowly he took his arrow and eliminated these suns, until Chang'e was able to convince him to let two remain as teacher and student, the Earth and the Sun. He was given immortality, which she drank instead so that he could remain on the Earth.

"The White Tiger had also come to this world with Goddess Danu. When she came from Metiorus, under the protection of Danu, to this world, she was able to release her Indigo and Pink Crystal being, and move into the incarnation of the Goddess of Love. She was given the realm of the Sun at first, but she was tired. The sun was always working to gift others through transforming their energy for them. As the Sun Goddess, she was fatigued, and so she asked Danu if she could become instead the Moon Goddess. It was as the Moon Goddess that she could create the shamanic path, and then have an ability to illuminate those on the path to transformation, rather than having to transform their energy. She had to leave behind a part of herself that became Father Sun, and she moved into her work as the Moon Goddess."

Chang'e is always with the Sun, even as she is the Moon, making sure that it never leaves us without the light. Of course, in Chinese constellations the Pleiades are Mǎo, the Hairy Head of the white tiger of the West. The head of Chang'e, the White Tiger, the Moon Goddess. Mǎo Xiù, the Hairy Head Mansion, is one of the twenty-eight mansions of the Chinese constellations, one of the western mansions of the White Tiger, also known as the White Tiger of the West. The White Tiger is often celebrated and worshipped on the 14th of the first lunar month, and so we will see if February 14 2022 packs as much in as January 14 2022 did. February 14 2023 for me was the gift of the heart, to remind me that love is the container of all of these channeled stories.

Her head resides in Taurus, the Divine Bull, and the Pleiades. There are three symbols and seven astrological "Mansions" within the White Tiger. Each mansion is associated with the position of the Moon. These include: Kuí or the Legs which are Eta Andromedae, Lóu or the Bond which is Beta Arietis, Wèi the Stomach which is 35 Arietis, Mǎo the Hairy Head which is Alcyone, Bì the Net which is Ain, Zī the Turtle Beak which is

Meissa, and Shēn the Three Star which are Alnitak. These will eventually be a new initiation.

We are told to start now with Eta Andromedae, which is where the bare feet of the chained woman are walking forward. She is walking towards the storm, or the bridge. There is a beautiful video on YouTube that you can find called, "Galactic Sound of Andromeda -: f=1/t Light Bridge:- by Cosmic Power Chord (432 binaural)" and it is the sound of a standing wave of light with power Harmonics between our Milkyway and Andromeda Galaxy. It is quite beautiful using the 432 hz ratio. Everything has to do with light and sound. We are made up of light and sound as these atomic beings. Albert Einstein said, "what we call" matter "is nothing but energy, the senses can perceive its vibration because it has been lowered, matter itself doesn't exist." We create the reality around us based on the light and sound frequencies that we tune into. This is where the law of attraction and the ideals of manifestation got started. When we start to look at sound as frequencies we start with A, which was named after Giuseppe Verdi, called Verdi's A. This sets A at the frequency of 432 hz.

The Law of Octaves is also the number 8. This resonating 8 hz is the number they say is essential for sound frequencies to create change in these created bodies for the human experience. Across the globe we tune our musical instruments at the frequency of A (432 Hz), and as such are obtaining adequate calculations with the so-called "Golden Scale". What this means is we will get a C (256 Hz) that due to the sympathetic resonance of the note overtones that will produce another C exactly to 8 Hz. Many of you may not know that the Great Pyramid is an eight-sided figure, and not a four-sided figure. This 8 hz is considered to be what creates DMT, as the frequency of the molecules produced by the pineal gland. It is also said that 8 hz is the frequency of hydrogen, and outside of oxygen that is what makes up most of our form. There is a reason why we desire the love song, because the frequency of love creates the greatest awakening of all.

Astronomers and so many others are now using data sonification where the captured digital data becomes translated into images, which is transformed into sound. Some of these elements of the image, like brightness and position, are assigned pitches and volumes, and that is what makes these symphonies of the universe. Other scientists are turning gravitational waves into sound waves as many of their properties are quite similar. All of these new techniques allow us in the human experience to experience their characteristics in a format that aligns to our physical makeup.

Eta Andromedae is not one star, but is called a Spectroscopic Binary Star where there are two stars although you cannot visually separate them. Dual lights, or two souls perhaps even so that we remember we are a soul in a body, and that we host the masculine and feminine energies. This star is a massive yellow star, and we moved from the solar plexus in the original two celestial codes. Although the Andromeda Galaxy is visible to the naked eye, it still resides 2.25 million lightyears away. The light we see from Eta Andromedae started its journey before Homo erectus evolved. Just another nudge from Spirit to note that these are very ancient code transmissions that have been specifically waiting for this moment to arrive.

Beta Arietis marks the Ram's horn. The sound waves from the Divine Masculine are coming through energetically even if you are not seeing that vocalization in your reality. The Lion roars.

Several thousand years ago Beta Arietis had the northern vernal equinox together with Gamma Arietis, and its name means "the two stars". Its name represents the lasso which was used to hang the sacrificed animal and the sickle for cutting down the harvest. Beta Arietis is coming to hold the sacrifice of the old masculine heart, and preparing to harvest the abundance that is coming when the rains start the harvest. The masculine may not believe this with the dust storm, which is something they have held onto since the Mayan civilization collapsed due to the lack of rain. In that time the feminine was sacrificed, which devastated the masculine heart. They have carried that wound since.

2200 years ago Beta Arietis was in conjunction with the Sun at the March equinox. The Spring Equinox is the return of warmth in our body and soul, the rebirth, the germination turns to the sprout. Karel and his wife Iris Schrijver, who co-authored 'Living with the Stars: How the Human Body Is Connected to the Life Cycles of the Earth, the Planets, and the Stars' have said that over 40,000 tonnes of cosmic dust fall to the planet every year, and eventually makes its way into our bodies. What has sprouted was perhaps in germination for the last 2200 years.

This star is called the "prime meridian" of Aries. This is the lifeforce and flow of the fire of this cardinal sign, but it also is significant for the new beginning. The other star point is called the First Point of Libra, even though that point now resides in Virgo. Remember that planet, and stars are as fluid to our daily life as we are to time.

Beta Arietis is a blue-white star, throat chakra and pure sound frequencies. The Root Chakra, Solar Plexus Chakra, and Throat Chakra are all aligned to masculine energies. I feel this is very aligned to Chiron, the wounded healer. Chiron will retrograde in Aries starting July 19 2022 through December 22 2022. Chiron entered Aries in February 2019 which is when I blocked my own masculine divine only out of a protective energy trying to keep my heart from opening up in this lifetime. Chiron in Aries puts us face to face with our wounds, which is a lot of what needs to be vocally addressed. However, it is important to note that Chiron will not move into Taurus until April 14 2027.

As I started the Divine Masculine Embodiment this week, it was so relevant to these codes, that I decided I had to share the journey with you. The Divine Masculine walked deeply through the veil. As the third eye clears, they are walking through a dark tunnel with an autumn glow on either side, which is a deep reddish-brown tone. The lightning strikes, and then a light appears on the right side of their path. As they get closer this light becomes the tears falling from the Divine Feminine's right eye. Again, the symbol of what we are seeing is just old visions, and that we are cleansing them with the rain, the tears, the water. Closer still and they see that the storm is within what the feminine energy is seeing today.

The Divine Masculine tries to tell the Divine Feminine their story, but their words are falling on deaf ears. The Divine Feminine is only focused on the approaching storm. Finally, they know, they must look at this through the feminine eyes.

The Divine Feminine is walking barefoot on the hard, dusty earth. She craves this approaching storm ahead - the rain, the thunder, the wind, the water all clearing away karmic energy stuck to her face and dried into the old tears. The Divine Masculine stands next to them, but realizes when he turns to look through his eyes, he doesn't see it. What he is seeing is a wall of dust coming towards them. He fears the dust storm as this new inner sight has just now opened.

The question that I asked was, "What does the masculine need to learn to allow the rain to enter the journey? Listen to the rattle and walk forward Divine Masculine. No matter the dust or the wind, the truth is now seeking your new masculine sight.

It is said that the light in the body is in the eye and "if thine eye be single, the whole body shall be full of light'. Inner sight, once you have activated it, cannot be undone. Even if I haven't used any psilocybin for a long time, which to be clear, I only was regularly using this as a minute microdose for healing my neural pathways from the loss of memory that I have seen in my mother. When I get deep into channeling, I feel the same feeling inwardly as when I am subtly boosting my DMT with divinely created plant medicine. We are the plant.

Over a year ago I started working with the Nakshatras, which are 27 lunar (sometimes 28) Zodiac signs that are attached to constellations, sometimes this is called Star Astrology or the Zodiac of Moon. The Nakshatra of Ashwini is the Aries burning hot sun. This is made up of those twin stars, Alpha Arietis and Beta Arietis. The ruling deities for Ashwini star in Vedic Astrology are the divine twin physicians. So, when you are pulled towards Beta Arietis you could have that deep calling of being a healer, but especially with the blue-white star you may work with light language or light and sound frequencies. Personally, I am very drawn to the light and sound frequencies in association to the DMT experience without requiring plant medicine for deep therapeutic support. Open up to the healing energies with your divine counterpart energy, and let it clear your water blockages so that you can flow.

We also see 35 Arietis, which is another Spectroscopic Binary Star in Aries, but is not a main star but a part of the outline. This beautiful blue star group is considered a Northern Star. I see this star energy as being the higher throat energy that is balancing out the lower tones. It is also part of the Musca Borealis, the Northern Fly constellation that is no longer recognized, but that fly in the ointment, that scratch in the throat to say what needs to be said. Originally that constellation was called Apes, the Bee, but this was hidden away with the productive energy of this star group long ago, until now. Apes is ready to pollinate again.

There is so much of what I have found in the Lower World in the spiritual energy of the forest. The Forest Goddess, Mielikki, from Finland holds the keys to the chest of honey. She is an Empress energy and we know it takes the Bee to produce honey, as an old esoteric teaching. She is also the one that gave Bear their claws. Bear made a promise to never abuse them. In the Pacific Northwest we have seen where the bears make claw marks in the forest trees, and in that mark grows a mushroom that protects the honey bee from the toxic pesticides and herbicides that are being sprayed. This goddess hid the bee from the world as we started to damage the bear, and destroy the forests. I see the bear in imagery in the tarot as Queen of Pentacles. She who creates the home. The Bee to me symbolizes the expansion of the soul. No one pays much attention to a fly, nor wants the fly to show up in their world. Except for my daughter. When she was about two years old, she made friends with a fly that we named Jessie. Jessie the Fly was her devoted friend until she was about ten or eleven and realized the lifecycle of the fly. This fly to her was protective, comforting, and took on many of the bee totem energies as he went on vacations, moving across the US, and finally one day near the end of fifth grade fell to the floor and died. Fifth grade was a pivotal point in both my daughter and my life in terms of our personal awakening of our dual energies within.

You may be called to remember that when we nourish our body with the sweetness of nature, that helps our cells communicate in the way that the bear communicates with the humble bee. This is about the colony within us, and is something very essential for these codes.

Alcyone, the Hairy Head, also called Eta Tauri, is located in the Bull and is the brightest star in the Pleiades constellation, and the third brightest star in the constellation of Taurus. This star is a fixed star which means its position is so distant that its motion can be measured only by very precise observations over long periods. We see it as being 00 Degrees on either side of Gemini. Aldebaran, Algol, Sirius, Arcturus, Antares and Vega are also all fixed stars. These I feel are meant to guide us to the codes and paths that we are moving towards. This is our knowledge base, Eta Tauri, and there is a host of Celestial Akasha being held in this star.

Eta Tauri is also known as Krittika Nakshatra, and is the Star of Fire. When we moved through the Fire Codes, we opened the knowledge base of this star where there is much spiritual and celestial information encoded. This star is divinely connected to our Godhead chakra point. As we open these Water Codes you will open the flow of information into this Alta Major Chakra node. Eta Tauri is a blue-white giant, and sitting behind our personal sound portal, this will change the way that you communicate. The New Zealand Māori have traditionally observed the heliacal rising of Matariki (Eta Tauri), as the New Year called Te Tou Hou. The official start of the New Year is then at the first New Moon after the heliacal rising of Matariki. The traditions that come over the next month are similar to that of Samhain, the Gaelic festival marking the end of the harvest season and beginning of the shadow work in the year. Matariki is again the symbol of the Protective Mother. She is the Protective Mother. She is Mother Spider. The original Shaman, the creator of Fire.

I wrote in the 'Celestial Spark' in the Aries channeled story: "*Unknown to you, your true nature is awakening.*"

This is happening to fire starters from all around the world. When Biliku comes to you, this is a great gift as she rarely moves from the outer worlds to share her knowledge. She is my Spirit Guide, who calls herself the Mother Spider, but she is the Grandmother of the spark of everything that sparks within us, and blazes externally. At the beginning of our time, after Chondrite launched his meteor at the earth and created life outside of the sea; Biliku came from the sky to rest on the warm rock below. It is said that she was part of the creation, helping to tie the stardust and gas together with her magic tiny intertwined nanofibrils of silk. She then is woven into the DNA of Alpamama herself, Mother Earth. She is both of the sky and of the planet, and as such she was birthed by the Cosmos and Pachamama before the portal was opened when the weaver was needed. Weaving was required for creation. (More of those ancient Andean rites.)

Biliku was as independent as your soul being, Fire Hero, and when she finished creating all that she had, she looked down at Mother Earth and then came out of the sky to rest on the warm rock, teaching the Serpent how to warm itself under Father Sun. Spiders have a passive respiratory system, which means when they have exerted themselves they must stop and take some time to rest and let the oxygen that was created when Pachamama helped spin and crush the Earth into being, wash over her lungs.

As she rested on her beautiful rock, she pulled a sparkling Abalone shell from the ocean, as a reminder that all life had sprung from the waters, the emotions, the love that surrounded the body of the Mother. She loved how the ocean was both torrential and calm. She too was a calm being, only weaving chaos when she is protective or when killing her mate. She comes to you with the ability to swing from Divine Feminine energy into Divine Masculine energy, and as such, you may find yourself now with a sort of Divine mood swing as you are starting your adventure. Biliku took the shell, and then pulled a rock from within Earth, lovingly stroking the body of the Earth Mother. She then struck the rock and with that spark she created Fire. Emotions and Fire being brought together to create the first passion on Mother Earth.

Even as your being is rooted in Fire, you may find that you are often being drawn back to the waters of the ocean. You are a fire starter, and the journey is about pulling the fire from below, and sharing it to above."

In 2022 Chiron is in Aries, so there is deep healing that this year is starting, and this is why the light grids are talking to so many right now. I feel this will play into so much more as we move forward. In 2023 that Spring Equinox Moon in Aries will probably go even deeper.

We are starting to work through the Celestial Light Grids, as Mother Spider is the creator, weaver, of all of these light grids. I see that the Moon Goddess has opened our higher pink heart chakra energy, which was slowly created with the magic of the stardust and love. When we reach the Pink Moon in April 2023, I expect a full on emotional collective intention to be set. When we pulled in the Water Codes, we pull it in through first the Alta Major Chakra on the Celestial Light Grids, and then as it taps into our prime meridians, we will need to pull out our Abalone shell, and pour the energetic waters onto the warm rock of our Solar Plexus.

Ain has come in just as the net, and it is not here to do anything but to guide us to its faint 11th magnitude companion that lies about 3 minutes of arc away from it. Their joining is hidden and they take at least half a million years to orbit each other. This star shines with the light of Venus in our sky, and Ain proper shines light during the near-full Moon. The star is most unusual in that it is also orbited by a planet. It is considered the Eye of the Bull, and it is "all seeing" in that magnitude. The planet that orbits these companions is now called Amateru, named for 'Amaterasu', the Shinto goddess of the Sun, born from the left eye of the god Izanagi. Just confirmation that this is keeping watch on the codes and the grids at all times.

Meissa is actually in the constellation of Orion. Again, this head of the hunter, gives this house two heads, and the duality of the mind. This star is pale white and violet, and gains its name from "white spot" which is the inner mind, the pineal gland, our third eye, but lands in the constellation behind the ear. This is the space where I see us collect old implanted energy that we've healed but not yet moved out of the body. When this area of our body is clogged, we do not have full access to our Alta Major Chakra. Meissa is also a binary star set that is 1100 light years away from each other. Orion's head has only three dim stars; Meissa, Phi, and Phi^2. They say:

"In his vast Head immerst in boundless spheres
"Three Stars less bright, but yet as great, he bears.

"But further off remov'd, their Splendor's lost." — Creech's Manilius (1st century A.D.).

This to me is the nod to the Golden Ratio that we are being ever reminded of in this recoding. Eventually the larger of the two binary stars will explode, and turn the lesser sized star into many white dwarf stars. This will happen when we are all fully recoded with the knowledge we need.

The final star that comes to this code is the Alnitak, the 33rd brightest star in our sky view. It is a triple star set in Orion's Belt. Alnitak is a superstar that radiates a 31,000-degree-Kelvin surface, and offers mostly ultraviolet wavelengths that are invisible to our human eyes. This bright blue star will give us the Water Codes we are seeking, as it largely holds this within its solar plexus hidden by Orion's girdle. Alnitak shines energetic light directly into the Flame Nebula, also called NGC 2024. This light knocks electrons away from the great clouds of hydrogen gas that reside there directed into the fire, the heart of the nebula. The Flame Nebula is a large star-forming region in the constellation Orion that lies about 1,400 light-years from Earth.

The Hubble telescope has now found that there is a dark, dusty heart in the nebula, where a star cluster resides, mostly hidden from view. The Divine Masculine sees the dust which is just where their heart has hidden the wishes to grow in this secret garden. The radiation from Alnitak's Golden Ratio star set, surrounded the codes with shields of particles, and these shields are also spaced at golden ratios to produce maximum deflection and protect the safe spot in the center of the Nebular. The radiation ionizes the Flame Nebula's hydrogen gas to release the Water Codes. When the gases begin to cool from their higher-energy state to a lower-energy state, it then emits energy in the form of light, causing the visible glow behind the swirled wisps of dust. The unconscious hearts see light, the invisible Water Codes are deeply connected to these hidden stars in the heart of the Hunter.

Heart Space / Barbara Christensen

"I'm in there somewhere, coming to life
When the day is dark
When my fear is high
I will hide within the space so deep
Where not even your eyes, can ever reach

For long ago, when we loved before time
There was truth around
My heart was high
Until I feel the water soothe again
I will stay inside and lock out the end

My love isn't dying
My love isn't cold
My love isn't something to lapse when
I'm froze
My heart is so sacred

Which you can never un-know
This heart is a vessel
Where these dreams can unfold."

Listen to your heart song, and you will arrive together with the fire and the water, harmonized in the space around the golden planes surrounded by the light of the atomic messages. We have moved through much of the later starseed codes including the most abundant forms that are seeded on the planet with the initial two codes. When you have finished these two recodes, they will bring you through the Blue Cyan starseed codes of Fire and Water. The Blue Rays are time and dimensional shape shifters, and they remember more the closer they get to the timeline shift we are moving towards. They hold codes within them that are meant to become activators for others for the rest of their time on this life journey. As Meteorians, which are Blue Rays I am told, you may have been cross created with Pleiadian and Sirian, Orion and Andromedan, Draconian and Venusian, Arcturian and Lyran starseed origin codes to be hidden in plain sight until it was time to activate.

Today, 03/04/23 (3,4,5) I saw the continuation of this cutting away what is no longer meant to be darkness in our sight.

Lietsu / Barbara Christensen

"I give away this rain
To serenade my heart
I let that spark inside me
Say goodbye ... we break apart

Flame from within guides me
Cleansed under the fjords
Where we'll pass beyond the water
Until we meet the sword."

The water has washed us clean. Eel is the divine union within. Strong, masculine energies abound within Eel as life protective. Also, Eel is feminine divinity following the cycle of the Moon Goddess, similar to the Hermit, Eel says take the time from protection, to delve into self-love. That means you have to address what is hiding in your thoughts.

In these next sessions we will open up the dodecahedron, the Air Codes to connect into the universe to your higher self through the ancient mystic mystery of you.

We are still in the last stages before the Age of Aquarius starts in 2024. We still need to wake the connection with the celestial thinkers. These you may think of as the Agarthan and Polarians, Anunnaki and Hadarian, and their deep shared genetic cousins, the Alpha Centaurians. They were here on the planet long before any of the other starseeds, and they have knowledge of the vortexes, time nodes and light forces that have survived through all time.

FOUR GUARDIANS

As I sat down to start the Water Codes, because they have been stalking me, I was reminded of the original journey with the bear in a red world. The journey has been a flow of storms. We walk towards the storm and as we move through the dust, moving towards the water we are transported to the Lion's Tomb in the Phrygian Valley in Turkey. We look up and see the fuzzy elongated river of the Andromeda galaxy, and the open star cluster of those Seven Sisters below sitting closer to the horizon. Polaris. Errai and Tadmor will become the new North Star set after Polaris A and B, and this is where the messages of the approaching storm started to be gifted to us. My guides say, "We require the water to cleanse the darkness. Let us move."

We have awakened our new hearts, and I am asked, "What is the fractal of pressure within the heart of the divine being?" They whisper to me, 'The next event we will see will bring the wind. This is a sign of silence. The inflow comes in from all directions, in a fast cycle of energy.

With a tornado, hurricane or cyclone the updraft comes before the storm in a supercell, a dancing spiral fractal. Madagascar, Malawi and Mozambique are currently cleaning up after Cyclone Ana, with caution that South Africa's east coast could be hit by intense tropical cyclones this year. The United States northeast coast is awaiting a bomb cyclone today as I am writing this story and pulling in these codes. This storm will unload at least a foot of snow, with minor flooding and hurricane-force wind gusts. She, Mother Earth, is cleansing, but using the spiral energy of creation from the Divine Feminine energy.

Spirit told me as I was channeling several months ago of the torrential rains of the year 2023, and while editing California was awaiting yet another atmospheric river, and yesterday

Tropical Storm Freddie hit Malawi. Our land masses are bring changed and this is just the start of the global flooding that will come.

This is why we are being shown the galaxy, as various codes are here to show us those celestial fractals. Hurricanes are spiral fractals as are agave cacti, sunflowers, shells, even one of my favorite plant proteins, the cauliflower. Fibonacci Spiral is a simple logarithmic spiral based on Fibonacci numbers and the Golden Ratio. This is also seen in the Golden Spiral.

The Fibonacci Spiral is the Empress, Creator, Pachamama, infinite in expansion, light. This is significant to the macro and micro cosmology of our lives. Everything is a pattern. The Golden Spiral is the masculine, Emperor, creating the cycles, breathwork, life and death, and universal law. The masculine energy inertly has opened the time dilation to connect outside of the force of this dimension. Our lives are always profoundly aligned with this law. We cannot out create the patterns, however as this is a fractal in the Chi energy codes, you are both what is, and what is unique. We are each a snowflake, in the most beautiful way. Or maybe you would rather call yourself the pattern on a giraffe. This is the silence within the storm.

It is the moments of stillness, the silence, where we recognize life's patterns, learn the lessons, and move forward.

Some days this requires a tornado or a hurricane to clear the old stagnant energy out.

The Feminine energy has been seeing the moisture and the lightning, while the Masculine energy has been seeing the Earth and the wind. Before the Tongan eruption the water started moving in spirals in a way they had never seen happen before. Right before the eruption there was forced silence, and on the island you could not 'hear' a thing.

The vortex at the Glastonbury Tor is very active right now opening up these water codes in the flow from the Cosmos and into the Lower World. They are being guided to us through these forces of the underwater eruptions and the storms. They are calling this the new Ace of Cups, the Holy Grail returns. It is not a coincidence that the storm that hit South Africa as I was channeling this code was called Ana. Ana, mother of Mary. She who said that the pyramids are machines, and our unconscious hearts will open their power. We have activated our new high heart chakra, and they are still yet a little unconscious.

In my journey space today, I was running through what felt like a tomb, almost like I would imagine it would feel inside of a pyramid. I was seeking the exit portal to get into the light. I was in a fire storm within. To get there I walked through fire, as my guides had taught me to do many months earlier. As I ran, one tunnel collapsed, and I ran in the opposite direction, finally seeing another tunnel. As I processed the early traumatic experiences of my childhood, Spirit reminds me of the way I escaped that space and the pain by creating a fire storm behind me as I escaped through the self-created tunnel of my soul fractioning off.

In the early 1800's a small village called Bogazköy was found 100 miles east of Ankara, Turkey. This town was identified as the remains of Hattusa, the capital city of the Hittites from ca. 1650-1200 BC. In the excavations they have found two sets of huge granaries where the grain was stored in massive rectangular silos. These were more or less pits dug into the earth. Upon further digging they found another structure, with mud-brick walls that were 1.5m thick. On the outside, this whole newly discovered complex was packed with layers of loam and clay in order to ensure it was air and watertight. So massive, measuring 118m long by up to 40m wide which is longer than a football field even if not quite as wide, it had thirty-two rectangular chambers in all. All of these in a double row. They dated it back to the 16th century BC, in the Old Hittite period. Twelve of the chambers had been consumed by fire when full and they said that excavating them was like excavating in a coal-mine. The mud-brick walls were burnt red, as the walls had been interlaced with timber beams. King Anitta from Kussara took credit for the act and erected an inscribed curse for good measure:

Whoever after me becomes king resettles Hattusas, let the Stormgod of the Sky strike him!

The Stormgod of the Sky, King of Swords, and that comes to mind for me today as Aries. Chiron moved out of retrograde direct into Aries in 2022 on January 11th. He was guiding us to look deeply at our wounded healer within. There is a lot of energy in these codes pushing us into that truth. On April 1 2022 as the Sun was conjunct Chiron in Aries, during the Aries season, it was like the sword was going inward. There is no running from this. The Sun melts the energy of Chiron within you, merging your being so that you must heal. Your wounds will show what a big part this has always been in your life.

The gold, the road paved to happiness, is the turning of the poisonous wound into your greatest medicine. I was shown the shamanic medicine wheel as the life cycle of clay. In it we worked our way through the Ego Death, where the East is our beginning as we enter each new journey, new story, or even new timeline. We move to "she who invites" who is the Wild Woman. Heart open, she is the Bone Collector that works through the dust storm to find those bones of animal and human and bring them back to life. "She who invites' smiles at me and says, she is Ana.

We move into the Nymph Fairy, whom Saturn rapes; which is where Chiron is created. She moves into the Praying Mantis,

Kamakiri, the mistaken zygote who has embodied her energy into the mantis to protect herself from the masculine energy. She leaps out of her life, sheds it as we must, leaving Chiron to create his own destiny. It is through Apollo that he becomes a healer rather than a monster like his parents. If there was ever a time of healing the old wounds of the Divine Feminine energy within us all, is it not now? Should we not also heal the deep fear caused by the abandonment of the Divine Masculine? Not just the masculine abandoning the feminine, but where the masculine has also felt abandoned. We cannot create from higher hearts if the two cannot fully be healed as one. Within each of us lies the two, and within every relationship synchronous system.

We then move to what they called "stomach art" which is the womb wounds of our Human Design, where we have been encoded and carry the desire to control and the fear of our past. This moves us to meet the Osaki, and see what ancestral spirits still reside within. Chiron still carries the deep wounds of his creation and abandonment, and it is almost as if he wills the arrow to find him so that he can show his wound to the world.

When you are in possession of these spiritual challenges, like the Sun Goddess, you may move into the cave, like the lone wolf, hiding your light, until illumination comes to your heart via the fire, and you are drawn out back into the world.

They didn't just find the burned-out grain reservoirs in Hattusa, they also found five huge reservoirs that were dug in marl, which was itself completely water-tight, so there was no further need for the insulation of the embankments. But though they were narrow, they were very deep – up to 8m – in order to minimize the loss due to evaporation. They believe some of these were for water storage. What masculine energy was storing up the emotions so tightly here? However, in one, they found a dump of more than a ton of clay pottery. They left all of the empty cups, perhaps in hope that one day they would return to love.

Back in the journey someone ran past me, and as I left the tomb and came out onto the sand. I turned and looked at this man, and he appeared to me as an old sailor. Our Upper World guides can be anyone, and to my surprise he appeared to be what I can only describe as Captain Hector Barbossa, from the Pirates of the Caribbean movies, whose daughter is Carina Smyth the astronomer and horologist. The movie captain was inspired by Hayreddin Barbarossa, an Ottoman naval captain operating in the 1500s. Hayreddin, or Redbeard, and he was the son of a potter. He died in Turkey. I know he was trying to direct me there as I was originally feeling that I was in Egypt since the Glastonbury Tor had already brought the red waters to me. The water runs red from the iron content. Clay is red because of the iron content. Interesting enough is that as my emotions washed over me, my iron stores were depleted.

In Glastonbury Tor the 13 zodiac signs line the earth at the Temple of the Stars, and Leo is where the Divine Flames, or Fiery Lions, esotericism is securely hidden. The lion's tongue is composed of red clay and is extended intentionally to rest on and point out the central line of the Ecliptic. It is believed that this layout was initiated from Egypt. This is wound into the fabric of the Water Codes. We started these codes aligned to the old North Star in the King's Chamber.

The three large pyramids, the Sphinx and the Nile, are a mirror reflection with pyramids honoring the three stars in the belt of Orion, the Sphinx corresponding to the constellation Leo, and the Nile corresponds to the Milky Way. Even before this time period the stone Calendar Circle at Nabta Playa that are hypothesized to be aligned to Sirius, Arcturus, Alpha Centauri, and the Belt of Orion. The southerly line of three stones seem to represent the three stars of Orion's Belt while the other three stones inside the calendar circle represent the shoulders and head stars of Orion. Orion's three belt stars also point up to red Aldebaran in V-shaped Taurus the Bull. It's the 13th brightest star in the night sky, and a sign map left for the union of the Lion's that made their way here so long ago.

Orion is easy to find and view in our February night sky. The Greek myth of Orion is that as a warrior he bragged he could kill all the animals on Earth. Mother Earth sent the scorpion to sting Orion's heel and kill him. Zeus rescued him, but placed him in the sky. Orion, still fearing the scorpion, only rises in the east after Scorpius has set in the west. Scorpio our sign for death and rebirth before Ophiuchus. I am told Ophiuchus should be our first sign of the Zodiac, like the East it is the new beginning. However, as the number, zero, like The Fool. Spirit whispers to me, only have Scorpius' sun has set, will the birth of the Empress rise.

The Pericú Indians that once inhabited Baja California, saw the three stars in the belt of Orion as the stones their God Niparaya used to descend from heaven onto Cerro Puerto, the highest peak to the west of El Sargento. Niparaya then created humans and all the plants and animals they would need to survive. Much of what these people would have built is long gone into the ocean, after the ice age. The Pericúes were tall and had significantly long, narrow skulls compared to other inhabitants of the area. They have determined that they are most likely to have come from Melanesia, known in genetic tests that you and I would have done from these online companies as Oceania. My daughter has 0.5% Oceania DNA, as do I. It is theorized that Lemuria once forged across the earth from Melanesia to Catalina. This makes sense as the Pericú share the same genetic lineage as the Australian aborigines.

However, some researchers have been measuring the skulls of ancient Brazilians and comparing them with these ancient

Pericú skulls finding that they are indeed a match. I think we should consider that the El Paraíso pyramid in Brazil may be 5,000 years old, and perhaps the oldest pyramid in the world has been found in Java, Indonesia, which would be part of the Melanesia / Oceania world, dating back over 20,000 years.

If these ancient Lemurians moved through Brazil, as I think they did, they could have left for reasons of climate and perhaps in Mexico and the Californias they found that they could not build pyramids, but it was easier to build caves and terraced homes. Cave paintings in Brazil have been dated back 36,000 years. Hidden Amazon settlements are still being discovered, although thousands of Brazilian pyramids have been destroyed by unregulated development. Scientists have recently claimed that a massive hailstorm from space bombarded the Earth 13,000 years ago along the west coast of Canada, and the United States, plunging the planet into a mini-ice age. This was caused by a disintegrating comet which sprayed the earth with thousands of frozen boulders made of ice and dust. These collisions wiped out huge numbers of animal species all over the world, disrupted the lives of our celestial ancestors and triggered a freeze that lasted more than 1,000 years.

I don't know what to do except laugh, because this week we had our own massive hail storms in the Seattle area. Interestingly enough, it was mitigated around my house, as well as the one other space where I long to be some days just to "see" the light. There was no light, just giant bombarding frozen boulders that I was sure were going to destroy my car before I could pick up my tiny traveler and be on my way.

Even if we consider how about every 20,000 years or so the Earth swivels on its axis, we don't know when it will happen. Six days ago, I channeled that we were off our axis as I saw the Animal Totems not sitting in their true directions and Serpent was swimming through the middle of the wheel. Tribal elders have been commenting over the last few years about the stars being different in the sky. Even 10,000 years ago Earth's top half was aimed toward the sun during the closest part of its orbit, which now is aligned to the Southern Hemisphere. All species on the planet are in constant cycles of migration because the planet is in cycles of constant migration. We are seeking this information now before there is another cycle that completes.

When we made our way out of the tunnel in the journey space, the building disappeared, and we were standing on sand. Although there seemed to be nothing but sand around us, there was a large tree that had fallen from out of nowhere, and my sea captain asked me to sit there. He pulled out a map and said, "Ay lass, let me show you where we are going." I thought that was a funny accent for my sea captain. He opened the map and as he was looking at it he turned his head upwards and pointing to the sky he said, "That be where we are going." I followed his direction to see he pointed to the large opening appearing in the sky. He said, "The Andromeda Galaxy, with the Lion."

As more information downloaded throughout the day, I realized we were in Hattusas, and the tunnel was located under the Lion's Gate where there was a pair of lion sphinxes at the southern gate. In the 'Celestial Spark' Aquarius Star Beings channeled story I said that when a hurricane meets a volcano on this journey, you could find your emotions intense. We have just had that happen. Cyclone Cody happened right before the Tongan eruption. This made it very hard to project the tsunami as the storm was altering swell height. We have to remember that the Spirits guided us that subterranean mountains are scattered all around the underworld. Thera, the Greek island of Santori, recently had four large scale eruptions that collapsed the island. Over 3,600 years ago the Minoan Spirit of the Divine Bull came to Aphrodite, and she swam away. After this recent storm and eruption, she also ran from the Divine Bull, which is why we are moving first to Turkey.

The area of the Great Temple located in the Lower City of Hattusa (the capital of the Hittite Empire in the Late Bronze Age). The temple was built in the 14th century BCE and was dedicated to the supreme deities of the Hittites, Teshub, the god of sky and storm, and the Sun goddess of Arinna.

Aphrodite is also considered to be the Goddess of the Sun. She is often depicted wearing a girdle, which Orion's belt is often called, And Aphrodite's main attendants were the three Charites. Hittitologist Volkert Haas has distinguished that there is actually a male Sun God, Ištanu. The female, Wurunšemu, is the Sun goddess of Arinna and spends her nights in the underworld. The feminine has been in the cave. We have seen this since after the meeting at the Axis Mundi. At one time Aphrodite had a love affair with Ares (Aries). But her heart belongs to Adonis, and it is this love triangle that ends in Adonis' death in mythology. She soars to him with her swan, but there is nothing she can do.

I returned to the journey space to work with Divine Feminine. I found them sitting in the cave, hiding their light in sacred rage standing with the wolf, still pure in energy. No matter how hard she tries to hide her light, even in a cave, just like it is for the Moon hiding from the Sun, her light is illuminating. She is seen. As she sits in the cave, painting on the walls, the mystic messages come into the mountain for divine healing bringing with them the Aurora Borealis. Still, she sits with Mother Spider, creating, because as a goddess of creation, she cannot break her soul purpose. She is embodied with the Great Divinity Illuminating Heaven, but the world cries for her light. Celestial light bringer, the dragon brings rain and snow to keep you in the cave for a little while longer, but even that will melt and nourish the harvest in time.

I believe that Helios, the Sun God, is finally trying to repay his guilt for Phaethon's passing. He has been showing up as the Atlas Moth in my journeys, showing that his chariot is being driven by two snakes, that are actually the moth. Helios is protecting the masculine energy, and their hidden emotions and hidden transformation. Aries, Ares, was Phaethon's father, and he died when racing chariots and getting too close to the son. You can imagine the wound of this strong warrior. For now, he sits in his cup waiting for the ability to speak their truth. They are working with the new hearts to bring the emotions in, pushing them to pull the chariot through the celestial ocean.

Outside the cave a mirror is created, waiting for the feminine to look in and see her truth, that she is light. The rains will bring the flowers and the flowers will dance along-side the bonfire coaxing her out of the cave. Do not be afraid, feminine. This is going to bring you back onto the new clay wheel so that you may see yourself, and have the heart to heart with her that is needed to awaken your courage. To have true union you must both align your hearts, even in different bodies. This is what will allow you to see that in eternity, there is no end and no beginning. It is all ever-unfolding.

The week ending before I edited this chapter, was a hard one. I was nearing the mediation that would end the karmic relationship I had been in for most of my life. Change is not easy, even when it is what you desire. Then I received and email that my therapist was no longer taking insurance, and I felt that deep wound of the feminine abandonment rises up and swell. The rains poured all day and night, and I awoke to a frozen deck from all of the hail that had come. I went into the sand digging and digging for my darkened heart, but it was tired, and done. I was ready to wander away and seek what I couldn't find, but it was there under the sand.

Recently there were 9,000-year-old agricultural tools found in the excavations in Istanbul where my sea captain died. The Hittites materials did not belong to the region, but showing they came to this region, fought, and when they won the fight, they offered gifts to their gods. They have also found Mycenaean tools and have found a settlement that has the traces of the Hittites, Cypriots and Mycenaean civilizations. I came out of the tunnel under the Lion's Gate, in Hattusa, and then we followed the stars. What they first showed us is that 9,200 years ago a massive solar storm hit the planet, with much of the force in the Northern European area, and that this caused mass collapse of various communication systems for the Lemurians. This is why their civilization collapsed, and they became nomadic and moved across the land. My communication on all fronts collapsed that weekend, and so I moved onto the oceans, as my emotions carried me forward.

We move onto the sea and he takes me to the ancient tomb in the Phrygian Valley. This is the Lion's Tomb, called Aslantaş, built into the volcanic rock of Turkey. It lies 11 meters from the ground, and the two mighty lions are depicted standing upright on their hind legs, as if preparing to jump. Their jaws are open, solidified in a silent roar. Between their silhouettes there is a square entrance to the tomb. Aslantaş is dated to an early period in the 8th century BCE. Built by the Phrygians, which are another ancient people we do not know very much about. They show up in prominence after the collapse of the Hittite Empire. There are tablets that have been found that show there was a treaty to end a long war between the Hittite Empire and the Egyptians between Ramesses II and Hattušiliš III. The treaty stated that both sides would forever remain at peace and bound the children and grandchildren of the parties. "They would not commit acts of aggression against each other, they would repatriate each other's political refugees and criminals and they would assist each other in suppressing rebellions. Each would come to the other's aid if it was threatened by outsiders:

"And if another enemy come [against] the land of Hatti... the great king of Egypt shall send his troops and his chariots and shall slay his enemy and he shall restore confidence to the land of Hatti."

The text concludes with an oath before

"a thousand gods, male gods and female gods" of the lands of Egypt and Hatti, witnessed by "the mountains and rivers of the lands of Egypt; the sky; the earth; the great sea; the winds; the clouds." If the treaty was ever violated, the oath-breaker would be cursed by the gods who "shall destroy his house, his land and his servants." Conversely, if he maintained his vows, he would be rewarded by the gods, who "will cause him to be healthy and to live."

The Hittite Empire dissolved, much like what we have seen in other ancient civilizations when the values splintered. The Minoan volcanic eruption that devastated the Aegean island of Thera (Santorini) happened around 1600 BCE. It destroyed the Minoan settlement at Akrotiri, as well as communities and agricultural areas on nearby islands and the coast of Crete with subsequent earthquakes and tsunamis. By 1250 BCE there was the beginnings of a 300-year drought that created a migration in all of these areas, and the empires started to fall.

The wanderers would have eventually made their way to Glastonbury, when the Celtic culture started to evolve as these travelers started migrating as early as 1200 BCE. This is where they came to, with Danu, the protector, as she again created safety for what remained of the star people under her watch. She has gifted us with the codes of Sulis, who is the eye of the Sun, the Sun goddess of Arinna. She who is hidden, illuminates light in the darkness. The "eye of the Sun" historically has been Ra.

As we moved towards the end of Aquarius season, the lion was pointing me to the Full Moon, the Black Moon, coming on February 16 2022 as the integration of the Water Codes. There are four guardians of the heavens. We have already met Aldebaran and Antares as being 00 degrees of Eta Tauri for the Fire Codes. Aldebaran also worked with Mars, the warrior planet of Mars and is the Eye of the Divine Bull. These two are the guardians along with Regulus, and Antares. Regulus is the brightest star in the constellation of Leo and will be near the full Moon to protect how we process the Water Codes. The fourth star comes from the "celestial sea" where Helios is driving the new dragon hearts that are transforming for the Golden Transmissions. All of the star patterns in this region have an association with water and include the constellations of Capricornus, Aquarius, and Pisces, and the star Fomalhaut became the fourth guardian.

It is actually a triple star system. Fomalhaut A was formed around 440 million years ago from a molecular cloud or a nebula, of gas and dust and has an exoplanet which was named

Fomalhaut b, also known as Dagon. Dagon seems to be around 400 million years old or even older, this suggests that the stars may be physically related, perhaps they formed at the same time and are now gravitationally bound to each other. Fomalhaut C is the smallest star, but much older than the other two. The power of three. A water molecule has three atoms. The four guardians will protect the codes until you all have accessed them.

When we access this code, we are going to call on the Black Moon, this is the full moon when the codes will be activated. You can call on these codes during any Dark Moon, calling on your inner Black Moon Lilith, the Wild Woman. These codes will be moving between many vortexes on the planet, but they will resonate from Glastonbury at this time.

This isn't just about the Emperor, the Lion. We are also connecting with the Lioness, the Empress. The Celestial Light Grids are playing a special role in this path, and after I journeyed to Turkey, I asked how to stay outward and expansive in our light?

Spirit showed me gathering light grids from the Heavens, but bundling them up like bundles of yarn. We are going to create something from these and I am meant to share this with you.

I felt a little possessive of the grids when I was first gathering them, almost as if I was afraid of spiritual famine. This is an old ancestral wound that the feminine heart is learning in regards to release attachments.

I went into a shamanic journey circle with only women. I was dancing around the circle with these women and our ancestors and the angels were joining us. I found myself looking into the soul of a wise Shaman elder that had just passed. I left the circle of women dancing around the fire in a ceremony of the seed. I am reminded of the vision that the cycle of the woman is seed, to womb, to life, to death, to seed. It would be months before I would realize I was invoking the magic of Eros and the Cosmic Seed. If you wish to hold your own seed ceremony, Sandra Ingerman teaches a beautiful ceremony where you just hold seeds in your hands. Speak or sing your soul song into your seeds, sharing your intentions for what you want to grow in this season. This could be perfect for a new moon ceremony. Then place your seeds in a pot or seed tray and cover them with dirt, or out in your garden and trust the elements to take care of them. You can spend a little time and hold your hands over the soil and send love from your heart sending them off into the world to birth.

I flew out of the circle as a dove and landed on a boat where I laid, floating on this almost black river, looking up at the sliver of the moon and then at the Southern cross of stars. It became increasingly dark and I saw one shooting white star which I followed.

I arrived at my destination and the wise Shaman elder told me I needed to now be initiated into the Raven medicine. It was a mystical energy of deep indigo, blue, black magic from Mother Earth. I was told I am helping to heal this earth, now. I was this amazingly bluish black "jay", the Amazonian raven.

As we left the sacred space the shaman turned into a massive lion that was unlike any I have ever seen. He took my hand and we shapeshifted, myself into the dove and he into the condor; and we flew above the most beautiful mountains and valleys until we came to the top of the highest mountain. There as a lion he took my hand and dug a hole. We placed my new moon seed into the ground and he invited me into my new seed. I crawled into the seed turning back into the dove. He said, "You will know it is time to grow when it is light."

I came back to the circle through the fire and we shared our journeys. One of my sisters floated in the water with me to the angels. Another met the wise Shaman elder before he went up onto the mountain to perform a sacred fire ceremony.

The next morning the Mother Spider Animal Totem card sitting on my Goddess on my desk, was tipped over. I knew she was ready to take a rest. I shuffled the cards and of course the card that jumped from the deck was the Lion.

That afternoon I worked with the masculine energies and he came into the channeled messages with the Lion. He walked into the session engaged in fire, wearing the blood of 1,000 centuries. This was very deep ancestral warrior wounds that the masculine had held onto. As the Lion fell asleep, the Condor came in and picked up the Lion like a rag doll and carried him across the plains. The Condor is what this elder shaman was known as.

The Condor dropped the lion into a portal, they said it was the Red Eye of Ra. It was calling in the Red Hematoid, which is a powerful root chakra activator to bring in protection and the warmth of Mother Earth like a warm blanket around him.

If we think about how the Sun appears red before a storm due to the dust in the air, it reminded me of the Red Star, Betelgeuse, Orion's supergiant. Twice since 2019 this star's light has diminished and scientists thought it was about to go supernova. It was actually spitting out stardust, a creation of a new world and a new life. I was told the Divine Masculine has a 400-day cycle of pulsation that starts now. This all aligns with the fact that the masculine energy has been approaching a dust storm in the channeled messages.

That night I went into the journey space to work with the Lion in the way that I had originally worked with Mother Spider, and when I met the lion deeply, I was introduced to the Lioness of God, Archangel Ariel.

The Lioness took me through the veil, breaking down the barriers between dimensions, realities, and periodically emerging quickly back into this body for a momentary tune up before whisking me back off into the strangest places I have ever been. I was like I was looking through the eyes of so many lifetimes, realities, dimensions, and traveling around learning.

We finally arrived in the Namib Desert and I walked barefoot towards the ceremonial space. We danced in and out of this space, moving through the eyes of ancient travelers until I could no longer .... be.

Awakened, I was sick from traveling. I now realize that this was all the water codes and I was in a manner of speaking, sea sick. We went in and out of this cloud of water vapor floating in space. This cloud is 30 billion miles away in a massive cosmic body containing at least 140 trillion times the amount of water in all the seas and oceans here on Earth. They call this a quasar, which is a quasi-stellar object, an extremely luminous active galactic nucleus, that is powered by a supermassive black hole. I realize that the black fire that I sent my old shadow energy into was a supermassive black hole. Black holes are black fire, creation of darkness into, well, I don't actually know. It's a transmutation that I imagine loops darkness into light into darkness again. The karmic wheel of the divine.

Quasars occur in the centers of galaxies where some host galaxies are interacting or even merging galaxies. According to New Quantum Results called loop quantum gravity that researchers Jorge Pullin and Rodolfo Gambini worked on we see these black holes differently. What they found was that just as the black hole began to squeeze tight, it suddenly loosened its grip again, as if a door was being opened. As you are pulled in, you would be spit out on the other side, showing that loop quantum gravity black holes are less like holes and more like tunnels, or passageways. For two hours in the shamanic realm, I was being moved through these tunnels and passageways like I was on a super collider ride at the amusement park. No wonder I felt like I did.

I cleared my energy into my volcanic rock and the salt. I laid down and it was like I was rocking in and out of my body. I spent 45 minutes letting that blessing of a man, Steve Nobel, guide me back into my body.

Fomalhaut has been connected with the angel Gabriel and is one of the four guardian (or sometimes called royal) stars.

Michael (Aldebaran) Watcher of the East.

Gabriel (Fomalhaut) Watcher of the South.

Raphael (The Healing Archangel Regulus) Watcher of the North.

Uriel (Antares) Watcher of the West.

Of course, Ariel, the Lioness, is the altar on which all of the directions sit. She is associated with all of the elementals being the caregiver of nature, the animals, the Earth and is considered to be androgynous as the duality of the archangel Uriel. The Lioness comes in as the seventh direction of the Heart chakra, connecting us to our soul's origin. This is why I was called to bring in the water codes through a channeled sacred cacao ceremony, to initiate our hearts to these deeply cosmic codes. The cacao ceremony is available on my website to those that are interested in this heart opening journey.

Link for information on this beautifully channeled ceremony: barbara-christensen.square.site/product/recorded-cacao-ceremony/73

When I got to this point of the chapter, I thought the chapter was closed, but this morning it reopened because it was clear that we needed to open our hearts. I am as much in need of this, as all of us, and we will not grow from the water that pours into the river if we do not allow the growth to happen.

I was taken to Israel, which is one of my oldest memories of my first journeys before I even knew that there was a word to describe it. I was told that when I came to Israel that this would be the space, I came to be safe. Safe from the torrential downfall of fire that was hitting this Earth.

Of course, I have seen that there is a sense of a fire storm that is coming from the Heavens, and this is where it is leading me in the water codes. When I went into the journey space today looking for gratitude, what I found was recognition. Recognition is the seed that we all must grow to open our hearts to that sacred garden within.

In my journey this morning I was told that I needed to give away a piece of my heart. My first thought was, "How dare! Haven't I given enough." In truth, it is the part of my heart that I have shielded from being a part of my walk-in life that wants to be set free. First the Great Greatest Grandmother came out of the veil of the rock, the 12,000-year-old shaman who had been buried in Israel near the Sea of Galilee. She was a giant of a woman, in my journey, but in this life all that is left is her bones showing she was merely my height, which isn't much. Buried with her over seventy tortoise shells, the wild boar forearm, the eagle wing bone, the marten skulls, the wild cow tail, a complete human foot and the fragments of a basalt bowl. This Natufian was showing me that the creek becomes a river, and that the dragonfly becomes the condor, the dirt of my garden becomes a lush forest but what it needs is the heart to grow into what it is meant for as a soul. The mind is superficial, while the heart is endless.

First, we open our hearts, then we rest.

So, I read that statement as I was editing, and it hit me. Like it had really landed in my life container. The Saturday before I had clawed open the space and cleaned it for the heart to land. Your pain is not your heart. So we have to open truly the heart space, which isn't easy, and then we can open the heart. Right now, collectively I feel we're opening the truest of hearts, and then and only then will we rest. It is all choice, which is Judgement, which is the Lovers, and which is the Fool. We choose, we love, we leap into the new and with the wings we've crafted we fly.

AETOS

When the Air Codes started coming in, Jupiter (enjoying time in Pisces) was kissing Venus; and of course it was no wonder why my energy desired that deep sensual kiss of the Lover's energy. As I sit down to write this, we are in the Partial Solar Eclipse as well on April 30 2022. This is a rare Black Moon, which is when we have a second New Moon in the same month. We also are moving towards the Eta Aquarid showers, a very powerful Mercury Retrograde, and a Full Lunar Eclipse. Now I understand why we had to wait until we were in the energy of the Eagle, the sign of the East, Cosmos, and sight to bring in these codes. As I am editing Jupiter is in Aries with a little square to Saturn, who just entered Pisces, and conjunct to Chiron. Spiritual discipline to heal for our highest vibrations. This has taken and cracked the concrete foundation of our life, to allow our last year to do that heart opening work and clear out the past sludge.

The East is the direction of new beginnings, and I am taken to the Star of Bethlehem. The space where the Star of Bethlehem was seen has been struck with three very intense astrological aspects. First this is where the birth of a new star, or nova in the small, northern constellation of Aquila in 4BC was recorded. One thousand years earlier, the code of Halley's Comet, was recorded in the same space. They may have been there at the same time, or the comet could have been leaving these sacred codes for the new star to encode on its birth.

The sacred Magi, or Three Kings, also we know saw something interesting in the sky as they left Babylon towards Jerusalem, in the same area where this new star was born, and where Halley's Comet was recorded. However, most believe this was actually the planetary conjunction of Jupiter and Saturn as we're experiencing that mini-square energy as they work together, at least a little bit. A year into the pandemic,

December 21st 2020, was the same rare conjunction of these two planets. We may be trying to clean up the mess that rare conjunction opened in our spiritual house. This was a rare conjunction called the Grand Conjunction. So special was this as it marked a 200-year period of Jupiter and Saturn conjunctions in Air signs leaving the Earth signs.

My friend, Louise Edington, who is a very talented astrologist, had written in October of 2020 that these were epochal times. What this means is we were moving into a distinct time that would be very important in regards to new developments and great changes. The month before this I started deep training into the shamanic approach to trauma healing. Three days before the Grand Conjunction, I joined the shamanic support group that has become deep members of my soul family. The first time I joined them on Zoom was the day after the Grand Conjunction in the energy marked by the Winter Solstice, the day we turn towards our rebirth. I couldn't turn away from the inner meaning for myself that these air codes are about opening up to our celestial family, and the path that we are following to get there. We ended our online support group unofficially with the 2022 Summer Solstice, but I have these deep soul ties for the rest of our lives.

On April 26th, at 7:21 AM PST, I worked through the creation of a magical talisman with Jupiter and Venus, and then let it marinade in the energy of their kiss. I am gearing up to go back into the work with the Astral Fire and cannot wait to see how that creative process flows.

Something to note here is that what you manifest, and how it comes through is not always going to be what you envisioned. The gift of our life journey is that alchemy of the unknown. I didn't realize how many unknowns were waiting for me to light that fire and begin this new cycle.

I had been delving into these lessons with Eros, the god of life energy, love and desire. Mars is intertwined with Eros, as it is the forename asteroid that mainly orbits Mars. Zeus has been associated with Eros - in many ways. Eros was a primeval god, son of Chaos, and yet also the original primeval emptiness of the universe that created Chaos and Darkness. If we think of this in terms of higher self and 3D self, higher Eros is the beginning of the cosmic birth, and then 3d Eros was birthed by the co-creation of Chaos and Darkness. It was only later tradition where Eros is the son of the goddess, Aphrodite, and Zeus.

Zeus and Jupiter are different cultures, but similar energies of the Sky/Cosmos Gods, which we also see as the energy associated with Eros. As I walked through the sky with these ancient codes, it was as if walking with time itself. All can be seen as aspects or each other in introspection if we move into our Twelfth House of Pisces, which is our divine completion of self in love, or union of divine love. Time is fluid, and we are always there to open the alchemy of divine timing. We are here, now, as you read this. It is your Divine Timing if you have chosen it.

Both Zeus and Jupiter have associations with the Eagle. The constellation of Aquila is meant to be Zeus' Eagle. Eagle served as Jupiter's personal messenger, as well. In both stories, this Eagle carries their thunderbolts, which is that flash of lightning accompanied by a crash of thunder. This was something that can only be described if you've personally experienced it. I have had the lightning, and the thunder, and I walk with the fire to the quickening that has yet to shake completely loose.

This is our pre-tower moment, and while writing these codes I went through what I now call the Awakening Tower. This is the moment your life awaits. We are collectively being shown that everything is changing, and change is the guide as we move into the Air. You cannot tame the wind, and the wind carries the messages of the Cosmos through us all.

This is the symbol to show we are moving into the Age of Aquarius. Aquarius is associated with the Greek myth about Ganymede. Aquarius is the Astrology House of the Collective. She was the cupbearer of the gods. Ganymede was taken by Zeus in the form of an eagle to be his lover and slave. During this morning's conjunction between Venus and Jupiter,

Ganymede, also the name of one of Jupiter's moons, was visible to the East. Our new beginning holds under the Moon the energy that now is the time to choose, slave or beloved to the energy of our fire. Which do we choose?

We place the cosmos into the state of light of the Sun, where the light is the being, and outside of it is where all else is becoming. We are the receptacle of this creation. The solar eclipse and the lunar eclipse are so important to these codes because they are not separate, the Sun and the Moon. They are also ever united in the trajectory of the micro cosmology drawn by the frequency into our inner knowing when we are aware of the moments of zero-point astrology. The Sun lights our fire, while the Moon helps us make sense of it.

It is only through working with the fire of the cosmos, as each planet expels its own fire into our cosmology, that we gain some movement of our soul path. Our own inhalation of the light of the Sun, is a channeling of fire within us. Like Jupiter it is fully expansive beyond what we think our life container can hold. It is, however, only through the simultaneous occurrence of action and passion, which is very much the wand energy, that we create. Starlight does not reach through the aspects of blocked barriers, but Astral light, which is in part sound waves, goes through any barrier. We are always reacting to the pulsation of the astral light, but it is the celestial barriers that impact our collective actions.

I went into journey space here, to exercise my energy to the subtle body life energy, to see what I needed to know about my own density in this celestial alignment. I was deep in the green healing light of the heart (something I had to travel to Iceland to understand) which then brought in the deep purple cosmos energy of the Raven. I was fine tuning my astral light decoder, so very 80's cereal generation of me, and this was allowing my third eye to be more aligned to the octaves of the cosmic energy. In my last journey I was shown that I have banded green light bands around both of my wrists. Like the red string, they are the focal point of love.

The Raven is Eros, as the master magician and holding transformative energy. He came in to teach me more of how to embody this shapeshifting energy of consciousness. When I had been initiated into the Raven medicine months earlier, I flew out of the circle as a dove and landed on a boat where I laid, floating on this almost black river, looking up at the sliver of the moon, and then at the Southern cross of stars. It became increasingly dark and I saw one shooting white star which I followed. It was that Star of Bethlehem, and I was also later able to connect this to the White Dwarf Stars in our codes.

The Southern Cross asterism is located in the constellation of Crux, the smallest constellation in the sky. It is represented as the Sun Goddess, and has been depicted on a stone engraving in Machu Picchu. The Incas knew it as "Chakana," meaning "stair," as it stepped into the Heavens.

Alpha Crucis, known as Acrux, is the brightest star in the constellation of Crux, and the 13th brightness star in the night sky. Around 2,000 years ago, the Southern Cross was visible from Jerusalem, and some regard Acrux as the star of Bethlehem that led the Magi to the baby Jesus. Again, this would have been even closer to the timeline, but I am again led to the idea that this was a stepping stone of celestial information that was being encoded.

Jupiter and Venus kissing today, and I felt into that energy as I was reminded that Jesus, if anything, was teaching us to be expansive in our abilities to love one another. Astrology.com wrote, "On the morning of August 12 in 3 B.C., Jupiter and Venus would've sat just 1/10th a degree apart in the dawn sky. That's one-fifth the diameter of the Full Moon. (The December 2020 conjunction between Jupiter and Saturn will have an identical separation, albeit in the evening sky.) That wasn't the end of the show, either. Venus and Jupiter continued their dance over most of the next year before finally appearing to merge into a single star in June." As I had my own great death the June prior, I can see the expansiveness that these months have provided me.

We are moving through the transformative energies that are coming into conjunction today with that magical kiss that happened in Jerusalem all of those years ago. The Ravens have been keeping these secrets about our soul purpose. We have been working through the transmutation of karmic energy to release our inner fears and return to the light. Raven medicine now awakens our energy of magic. If Raven dropped out of the elements to create the land mass out of the "water", the harmony of sound, then this is the sound of freedom available to our thoughts most of all. This is the astral light of Venus that is bringing us an astrological song of the heart today. Raven, the great black hole, the great mystery of the void, that which is not yet formed.

Our hearts are this black hole of the Raven medicine. Our hearts cannot have blood in the atrium and the ventricles at the same time. A black hole collects materials to heat up (corona) and then spits it out in jets. I was asked to look at the constellation Aquila, the Eagle, and as I did, I was shown 36,000 light years away in the Eagle's direction was the black hole GRS 1915+105.

This black hole is a stellar black hole, giving you the power of the stellar fire of creation. Chaos lives in the EMF as the black hole heats up, and the less chaotic energy is the jetting of the energy field lines that it sends out. Researchers out of the Netherlands developed a cosmic echocardiogram graph, showing GRS 1915+105's "heartbeat". A heartbeat would lead you to believe that this is about the creation of love now that we have healed our water codes.

This is not an isolated black hole, but rather it is a black hole and a star that circle around each other. A light (live) star, and a dark (collapsed) star. The single live star is our guide, and the collapsed star is our guide to healing the karmic and becoming love. The closer you get to unraveling the stuck memories within your cellular body, the more you will feel your own heartbeat. Some days don't you feel it pounding out of your chest as you're bringing the deepest wounds to the surface to heal? This is something I have experienced moments before coming across the path of a divine energy in my universe. Eventually you will feel yourself standing at the crossroads. It is the moment you decide who chooses your path. Do you let the egoic memories, or the transformative soul make that decision?

This is old energy and new energy bound together. Does that sound familiar?

Memories are attached to our limbic brain, the neocortex that we are rewiring with these codes, and our journey work. The amygdala, which is an important part of our limbic system, innervates the autonomic networks and produces that change in heart rate as a visceral sign of emotional arousal. Your heartbeat is more than just the fight or flight system, it is the knowing within. The mindfulness practice reduces the anxiety associated with this system, which opens you up to a different practice within your path.

As we lower our autonomic reactivity, we are creating collapsed realities, opening to see the possibility that was previously hidden in our heart.

One of the most amazing things to know about the black hole is that it itself is invisible, but the gaseous matter pouring into it from the live star is exceptionally visible. We don't often see what gift is being given to us, as we are only looking into the shadows that we are working through. The gift is deeper in the heart than we can see. That space is invisible. The gas spirals into the black hole like water down a drain, and the deeper we get into our shadow work the darker it may feel. We lose track of time, as the life being sucked into the shadow, like the black hole doesn't just fall in all at once. This gas spirals first swirling around the black hole, forming a reservoir of matter called an accretion disk. The spiral energy is our feminine energy, which we all have.

Gas in the accretion disk gets extremely hot and emits light across a wide range of wavelengths. The inner part of the accretion disk, closest to the black hole, can be particularly bright in these types of systems. It is no wonder that the closer you get to the core of your heart, the darker you will feel and then the more autonomic reaction will come up to the surface. You are working through the release of memories, shadows, created by the gravitational pull of your nearby collapsed star.

One of the most important parts of this code, is that place where matter is compressed down to an infinitely tiny point. Here all conceptions of time and space completely break down. This point is the nothingness that spawns the something, which we can only call the in between. I created in my last three tarot decks the card that represents between The World card 21 and The Fool card 0. Not quite singularity, but if we compare what we are seeing with the black hole and with what was described as Tzimtzum, then perhaps the black hole is a mimicking of creation, guiding us to what we believe has an end, and yet is endless. Jewish mysticism believes that the black hole in some way connected with the supreme dimension, the crown or "keter"; as black represents the "primordial darkness", our Eros. The other side of that is the limitless light of the divine, or Infinite, no-end, known as the "Ein Sof".

Our Divine Masculine energy is trying so hard to get out of the loops of the mind, and into the birth of the heart. The only options however are bound together. Here we cannot be light without being in allowance of the darkness.

This came through in my journey with the circle of women I journey with twice a month, who I call the "Moon Ladies". We were journeying with Venus and Jupiter and I went into the underworld floating in a canoe. Eventually I came out, as a Dove, and flew into the Sun. The Dove pulls Venus' chariot, and again it was an alignment of the light and the darkness. We need that darkness to lead us to the light.

When I was journeying during the creation of my talisman early one morning, I also was guided by the Dove and the Eagle, bringing in the Animal Totem guides of Venus and Jupiter. Dove is symbolic of birthing hope, and peace when we are ready for the messages that we seek. Being in the space of peace with these messages feels very magical, and as if we are about to create something beautiful out of the last several years of chaos and darkness.

GRS 1915+105 is the heaviest of the stellar black holes so far known in the Milky Way Galaxy, and it may not be surprising to know that it lies on the celestial equator of this galaxy. I was about to enter this void, and I did not know it.

Before I talk about the Void, I want to talk about the journeys that happened after the Void with Hank Wesselman. For those that have read "From The Diary of Woo", you know I never met Hank in this realm, but instead only in the Ethers. He taught me that the rainbow is made of stardust, and light; which is what we are made up of as well. Energy, wind, fire, water, and earth... together these elements serve us well.

Last night I had Hank come to me and he took me on a journey through an open circle in New York City. The room was large, and there was a wall where we were able to hang our coats in the back, and I also hung up my backpack that I had been carrying and not wanting to give over to the seagull in the evening journey a few days before.

We sat in a circle, most of us on the floor and several on chairs, and Hank stood in the middle and opened the circle. He created a fire pit in the center. He told us as he moved to the direction of our hearts and reminded us that we are reflecting our hearts to each other in this space, and that we should remember that. He asked us to pull our bowls of light out of ourselves and they seemed to come from within the fire center, from the space of the sacral chakra. We each had some stones in our bowls. The fire started and he reminded us that as we share our pebbles with others, do not attempt to place your pebble into someone else's bowl. When you want to release the stone, place it in the fire instead.

When I went back into the journey after the circle, my personal sacred space, I walked with Hank again, but I was walking barefoot on the sand. This sand was like glass. It was hot and the Sun was beating down on us. Hank took my hand with his big "workers" hands and led me into a slot canyon with tall walls the color of sand with red streaking through it, like the blood pulsing through our veins.

We came to an entrance to what appeared to be a cave now, but was a man-made room within. We sat in the middle and he brought to my attention a beautiful bright white shaft of light, or white kundalini fire energy, that not only came through the top of my head but surrounded the entire space where we were. This is our life container.

Hank picked up what appeared to be a small skeleton hanging on a string, and I realized that it was many bones strung together in the formation of a body. He started tapping on it with a stick, moving it around me like he was doing a healing ceremony or a tuning ceremony with the bones. He then played my head like it had been turned into a crystal singing bowl by the light. It felt like a sound bath, and I could feel it pulling painful energy out of the back of my lower teeth, my jaw, and then my biceps.

It then became dark. In the darkness I found that I was no longer in my body, but was instead in the body of a jaguar. Hank walked me out of the cave, and we were on a path in a very lush forest. We were standing on one side of a mountain, and across from us was another mountain. The sky behind the other mountain was a darkened dusty red hue and he turned to me and said, " The Fire is coming. Tell the People to run." I don't know if he was talking about us making soulful strides, or if we are being warned that now is the time to prepare for something bigger.

Later I went back to talk to Fire. I went into my garden here in the Seattle area in Discovery Park. In the 1800's the land became a military fort of the United States, and was maintained through WWI, WWII and the Korean War. In 1965, one hundred years after the US-Indian treaty had promised that Fort Lawton would be returned to the original land owners when it was no longer needed, a deal was reached where Seattle would get a public park on a 99-year lease.

This park holds such a beautiful energy for me, and I went there to my sacred garden on my journey, and created a space for the Fire to come in to teach me. First is a forged a turquoise necklace that the Fire gifted me with. The Turquoise Lord, Ziuhtecuhtli, was the Old God of Fire for the Aztec people. Once every 52 years, at the end of a complete cycle in the calendar of the Aztecs, fire was ceremonially transferred first from temple to temple and then from temples to homes. I find it fascinating that I was 52 when I started my Shamanist journey as a Keeper of Fire. It is a very porous stone, and so as a talisman it becomes an extension of the one who holds this stone close to its body. I am deeply connected to this stone and as I am learning in these circles, I am absorbing knowledge that will help me weave together my gift of storytelling for others. Fire said, "You are a storyteller."

Fire then became lightning, which is often seen as a call to your shaman experience. Lightning is the meeting of hot and cold, so above and so below. This is the essence of what I see as the Tower energy in the Tarot Major Arcana, Energy unlocking emotions, and can be used to destroy and burn down what idea are no longer serving us to create space for something new in life. I had been struck, dead for a moment, and reborn several days before in a metaphorically speaking event. This is what had to be destroyed for me to have that moment of awakening.

Then Fire danced, showing me that it was never really contained in my fire pit. It showed me that it was also in the power of the stars that resides in us all. I saw it brought to the planet by what I can only call a UFO, and when we seek Fire, we are seeking our inner truth of who we are. I looked around for Hank, and saw him walking out of the ocean with flipper feet, and the ocean creatures were sad to see him returning to me. He showed me that we had visited all of the homes of Atlantis. The stars above, the sands of hidden villages, the lush mountains of the Atlantean world, and then in the underwater volcanoes far below in the depths of the Ocean. He showed me that my yin-yang is fire and water. I can work with these elements at all times, and that we must trust and believe in the

Fire of our Star People. We are shifting and changing who we are in this world right now.

The cards that I pulled for my circle today started with The Serpent and The Corn, both numbered 10 or 1 at the core. We are manifesting the shift, and the shift is of a new earth. We are the Keepers of the Earth, and the Gatekeepers of the Elemental forces. Our ancient ancestors stand beside us, and we are not meant to be fitting in. It's not quite time, we know, but time is being woven and the portal is being crafted. Just wait for that. For now, we are Earthed, learning to be human-souls, yet calling in our Star Family to feel complete.

We are told that this is a personal choice. The elements like the spirit totems are always able to gift us their qualities when we've learned how to work with them. Be brave when it comes to the way we fear our emotions. Losing cities deep into the sea, it forced us into human existence and that forced us to learn to work with Fire again. Now is the time to act, and open up to the opportunities at hand. There is nothing that we cannot accomplish if we just believe.

I look back to GRS 1915+105 as it shoots strong jets of electrically charged particles into space from just above the black hole's north and south poles. These jets are fed by material from the accretion disk, which is the gas, dust and other stellar debris that has come close to a black hole but not quite fallen into it. These elements form a flattened band of spinning matter, and that is what is called the accretion disk. It reminds me of the Soul Space being flattened so that we could enter this space. In the birth process of effacement, the cervix flattens, stretching and thinning so that the baby can be born through the birth canal. The rings around Saturn, the Lord of Karma, are also accretion disks of our story today. Time is fluid, and so it doesn't matter when you read this, just know that you are going through a transformation.

Think about the fact that accretion is a process of growth. This massive object is gravitationally attracting and collecting additional material, and that is what we are doing energetically with the yin-yang of our own push and pull. To rewire our limbic brain, we have to find the way to remove the obstacles, the darkness. We pull in and attract the material to grow. It is no wonder that as I am typing this, I stop to return a call to a friend and she is at the Museum of Flight in the Space Room. It was the time for these codes to be written.

I am also writing another book currently called, 'The Awakened Heart'. In this other book I share, "The mirror soul opens the void to fall into and fall away from this part of the physical body manifestation." So, what is this void?

The Radiant Body of our Kundalini plane is light energy and we partially understand this in the work in biophotons. The void, is the empty space or is the space where magic of living happens at a level we try to push away from. Being fully aligned with your light isn't easy. The photon hypothesis suggests that we are light, and that our light gets released from chemical processes, that neocortex loop, within the brain producing biophysical pictures during visual imagery. Recently there was a study that found that when subjects actively imagined light in a very dark environment their intention produced significant increases in ultra-weak photo emissions.

This is aligned with what we know about biophotons as they are not solely cellular metabolic by-products, but rather energetic creation. This is because biophoton intensity can be considerably higher inside cells than outside. Just as we find in the black hole. It is possible for the mind to access this energy gradient to create intrinsic biophysical pictures during visual perception and imagery. This is the journey space of imagined knowing, and the woo of carrying around the information you are seeking. As Rumi said, "What you seek is seeking you." Like attracts like, but even more than that as my Mindset & Affirmation card of "Wish" states that the subconscious mind can be sending out those intentions that you don't even know you're sending to the universe.

Every cell, every bit of your DNA stores and communicates with this light. Every single cell. You are a flame, an emitter of life. As well, the Sun, that massive emitter or light that warms our being, is communicating with you through your skin. Father Sun is seen in shamanic work as they see the melanin cells convert 99.9% of ultraviolet light into metabolic energy. This aligns with the knowledge that all atoms are 99.9% empty. What wisdom is the Sun imparting to us? What wisdom is it imparting to the foods we are growing to eat?

I went into journey space to find the aurora borealis, and it started as singular strands of light. When I reached the Lower World an orange fox came up and nipped on my jacket to follow. It took me down a path following the lights until we came to the edge of a cliff perhaps in Scotland or Ireland looking off into the ocean. I asked the fox what I should do and it pushed me off to dive into the ocean. I love that Fox has been coming into my journey space. Fox can be the dark, shadowy side of our woo, but also supports us in creatively dreaming up adaptations to our older and outdated codes.

When I came up from the ocean a man picked me up into the air and twirled me around. I was a toddler and he was my father at that time. He held me cheek to cheek. When we went back to our small home, like a small little house in the prairie home, he sat me on the floor and left. My mother held me while I cried.

I have worked so many lifetimes to understand that when someone leaves me is not a reflection on the love, they have for me. This was something I had needed to heal for myself, and for generations of children, partners, friends and lovers.

I went into the aurora borealis and I saw the eyes of my yang. At that moment my yang was in their lone wolf energy, seeking and growing. Pulling from me, flattening me so that I could be rebirthed. I went into the Void about a week ago, and in that space, I was completely flattened. Everything that I had been and everything that I had known up until now about love, and loving myself shifted in that moment. I truly for several hours felt as if I had died. In truth, this was a mirroring of the mess that happens when two black holes collide.

I could feel the heartbeat, in the low energies from an accretion disc the heartbeat was present. Slowly my heart was beating in the darkness of the different caves, and the two black holes were mirroring this. Even if two black holes collide, I am reminded that the accretion disc still sustains. So even in the mess of speaking truths through the mess of texts, it was truths, and love, and hurt all in the same space, but different spaces of darkness.

The lesson for me through sharing, is that saying a truth doesn't require anything in return; by just letting the truth be what opens the door of your hard prison cell. I had locked my inner child's heart behind a huge void in protection. Yes, as a child who could not protect myself, and that was the answer the Great White Eagle gave to me. A space to hide away from the abuses that no living being should have to live through. Then the Jaguar pushed me into the darkness of that void so that I could fight to live in the light. Very little grows in the dark, despite most of our reality being dark matter, yet the darkness can be what is most beautiful about you when you illuminate that cave of your heart.

At some point last year, Hank, I believe, or another energetic Shaman working with Hank, threw me into the darkness of an inactive volcano. At that moment my expectation was that I wouldn't survive. But when I let go, I floated like a feather to a solid surface. I have created expectations that others cannot reach. I have set out expectations that are meant to keep me in a fear and failure mindset. Yet I am not that. In this I can see that I am Luna Lovegood, I am Samwise Gamgee. I believe. I am a believer. But maybe what I can see isn't meant for anyone else and I am just writing this as therapy. That is the part I have yet to explore. Could it be that what we see through our Eagle vision is only meant for us? Perhaps it is all the tree falling in the forest. Can any one of us just open up and be, and not change the entire world around us? I feel this is the sacred medicine that Aquila was opening to us, and it was going to ripple around the Universe, and I truly hope that it will.

Seeing your truth takes a great, bold energy to allow that to come forward. It is a space where you reach within and let all of the fear go. That is the essence of this code. We aren't afraid of colliding, we aren't afraid of imploding, we reach that infinity point. You have rebirthed a new heart, but it comes at the cost of creating a new life. Life is created as a co-creative aspect. Even the singular cell is aspecting energy.

For Saturn's return, or retrograde, I asked the Moon Ladies to do a journey so that we could each bring a word back to the group to explore. Saturn retrograde is all about lessons to be learned and karma. We often forget that the idea of the retrograde season is to look back at what needs to be gone over again to really be cleared and understood. Saturn, of course, is a strict teacher and can give us a chance to really learn what you need to at this time.

So now the backstory of the backpack. In my Saturn Return journey I was directed by leopards to go to the water where the seals were swimming home like the local salmon do here in the ladder on the Puget Sound. There was a rope bridge over the water that I had to walk across to get to an island. As I was crossing the bridge, I realized I was carrying a backpack. This wasn't something I realized until a seagull tried to steal it. What baggage do you carry that you don't even realize?

My friend, an amazing energy worker, told me a story about how she had pulled this energy out of a woman that was so long and so deep that she enlisted a tree to help her retrieve it.

The woman told her several days later that she didn't know what she had done, but for years she had carried the greatest burden around from the way that she was treated by others. The burden, she said, had disappeared. She couldn't explain how light she felt. As she was being thanked, she said, "Don't thank me. Thank the tree." This woman, who carried such a burden, had only just convinced her neighbor to not cut down the tree. Life is co-creative. That which you are in thought of, is painting and creating with you. There's more to it than we see in the singular moments.

On the other side of the bridge on this small island was a large silk swing, like the old egg wicker swings, just hanging there. I crawled inside of it and was transported into a cocoon and was told I was 'molting". Molting is when birds shed old feathers, hair, or skin, or an old shell, or when the snake needs to release old skin to make way for a new growth. The Serpent lies in the direction of the South. As I asked my sisterhood about their take on molting, it was shared that many birds molt seasonally in the Spring. This aspect is to get rid of the old (no longer usable) feathers for renewal (new feathers come in). Seasonally could be seen as those times when we come out of the darkness, and into the light.

Of course, the Jaguar and Leopard are in the West, where we hold the emotions, the water energy, the illumination of the Moon, and I was being taken to the ocean by a very strong power animal that was a beautiful symbolism of renewal. Even bringing with it the cleansing energy, a washing away, or perhaps purging by the powerful pull of the waves with the lunar cycles of the Moon in this direction. I look at the turtle's shell as it is also the lunar calendar of thirteen. Leopard symbolism reminded me that there is always a period of rebirth after a period of radical change. Thus, this spirit animal is the healer of deep wounds. In other words, Leopard's gift was bringing old issues to resolution through the reclaiming of my lost power during the time of the wounding.

Our beautiful spirit guides, the Seals, are also considered to be powerful totem and spirit animals. They can be symbols of good luck and are very closely tied to our dreams, emotions, strength, protection, and movement. In my journey they were going upstream to spawn and create new life. There they would fight the currents of the stream with a great effort to spawn and in that act, almost definitely primal, as it is their final act and afterwards, they die. Like the Eel that would come to cleanse my heart space, who travels 3,000 miles just to mate once, breed and die. We are in a primal movement forward that you might not even understand.

Again, a necessary death of the old in order to have the birth, the old must give way to the new. Seals are agile; holding a fantastic gift at maneuvering through the water, even when the tidal waters shift and change. On the human plane, Seal's ability to navigate deep waters is equal to your ability to adjust to new circumstances and to remain comfortable with the ever-changing energetic tides all around us. With the Lunar and Solar Eclipse that we had just experienced, we had been through some massive changes. Change means we have to move out of the old, self-defeating circles. We will have to overhaul the old thinking patterns if we are to find our way.

I was "crossing over " leaving one space for another, and the seagull in taking away/attempting to take my backpack may have just been an indicator that we are carrying too much. That the seagull is trying to lighten our load, or just a reminder that we no longer need to carry this baggage. In fact, in the afterlife, we leave it all behind. Even our hearts cannot come I was reminded as I went into the cocoon almost protectively to re-emerge into a new life form as safely as possible. The seagull totem is a powerful symbol of a new dawn and was nudging me into moving out of your comfort zone, letting things go. This coding is a strong energy of transformation and transmutation.

Remember that when things seem like they are meant to derail you or to halt your progress, the truth is that these experiences are meant to fortify us in our journey. The seagull says, "Hey, let go and cut off such things that will weigh you down". This is the only way.

Another beautiful member of the group read us a beautiful poem that was called, "The Impeccable Path". What does it mean to be impeccable? To be free from fault or blame. Fear is something we create when we feel we are at fault, or another is at fault, or we are looking to blame why we cannot move ahead. What if there is no wrong path? What if every path is what is meant in the moment, and thus all choices are impeccable and hold no fear? This was an amazing space to move into our continuation journey with.

I was taken by Eagle to the Upper World where Thomas Kinkade was awaiting. He told me that here, the afterlife, is where we will all eventually end up. That no matter the path, it ends up here.

Thomas Kinkade had me lie down on train tracks and as the train passed me by, he said, "See. Underneath it is all the same. The inside of the cars may be differently done, and the trains going to other places. Yet the caboose always comes around."

He said our hearts are like everlasting gobstoppers, except everlasting seeds. When we move to the afterlife the only part of our journey that remains is the seeds we planted with our heart.

What about those seeds? NASA says that black holes are grown from seeds. The idea is that supermassive black holes have grown from a population of smaller black holes that has never been seen. This seed black hole is a black hole at its initial stage, like the infant stage in the life of a human. The baby black hole perhaps grows much faster than the supermassive black holes do.

Fixed star Altair, which is the brightest star in the Eagle, at 1º 47' Aquarius, comes to me as quite a collective energy. As a dwarf star, it has exhausted its fuel and the only thing that remains is the hot core. When the white dwarf star finally hits the point of no return, it will explode in a violent supernova, possibly spawning these baby black holes. So, this being central to the Eagle is pointing to us that what dies, also rebirths, so that we can continue to be open to growth while releasing fear. This is the cycle that we go through when our heart explodes as our deepest fears of the lessons, we have been holding in the head finally happen in the heart. This is usually due to a blockage in the throat chakra and this happens when we can no longer hold in what must be said. Altair is the neck of the Eagle in the Aquila Constellation. Collectively your thoughts are going supernova. How are you aligning to speak in truth, but without the post Mercury Retrograde energy that boils within.

Energy will seed, after that supernova, and what will it pollinate, grow, like the Ætihvönn, the Icelandic Angelica herb that was sought out for its healing arts connected to the Holy Ghost. Hank Wesselman called the Holy Ghost our higher self, coming out of the Paqarinas, the inner cave, where we reach the space of truth. Moving out of the shadows of the inner cave, and seeing what is real surrounding us. You may think that what you are being called to plant, decided in your head space, is the big glamorous idea, but it comes back to you when you leave the cave as something small that travels far. It may be even more important than you give it credit for.

In my journey today I was taken by Mother Spider and my guides to dance around the fire. My guide turned into a big, brown bear, and I was asked to follow. We walked through the forest path and I turned into a fox. I was curious, finally, rather than being decided. Decisions are the limitation of our soul, because we block the path from opening up to something else. The bear stood up, and he was mightily powerful, and scratched his claws deeply down the side of the tree. Reminding me in that moment of the fungus that grows in those claw marks is like a superfood for the immunity and protection of the honeybee. You are an important part of the pollination of life. We were also being taught how we all have a part of the pollination that is created in this Universe.

As we continued on, I found that the bear turned into a bee, and so did I. We followed the music, the harmonized energy, to another teacher of mine who works with the soul through these harmonies. I landed on her nose, and she reminds me often to smell the energy of what I am envisioning, and that is a strong force of creation.

I became the fox again, and I was following the focal frequencies back on the path, but now we were going into the heart. My heart, which had been reborn, was a little cold. I was walking the path in the snow in Iceland. However, I keep seeing the beautiful blooming green flowers that were calling to me, this was the ætihvönn, angel herb, angelica. This beautiful herb survived the Ice Age, and thrives throughout Iceland. The roots were once used as currency among the Icelandic Vikings to trade with other countries. The flower, leaves, stem and seeds all hold special medicinal and therapeutic qualities, but it was the energy that was calling to me. It is a protective energy, and used to soothe our throat, soothe our inner cave, our inner critic. This little green flower, hidden away in the darkness of this tiny island, like the cave of our world, may be the beauty that the world needs right now. A little connectivity to our higher self, removing negative energies, and opening up our heart to bloom.

I was shown that we are the creators. This air, which is our thoughts. If you write in your head or your heart what it is that is wrong with you, you close up like an oyster. Inside of you is that pearl of wisdom that balances out the karmic lesson, but you have to open up to see it. When you do, you can change the page of your story. What if you wrote down the things that were told to your head and your heart, and turned them into butterflies instead. Can you see that in the caterpillar soup these were hurtful expressions that you placed on yourself. Yet when you release them from the cocoon, they become something special that delights your senses. Transmutation is always going to return all energies to zero. Zero, which is more powerful than we consider.

Metamorphosis happens with many animals that we engage with. When I was last taken to the fire, I was shown that we've all reached a point in life where we have called in fire to create a transformation. We have seen to the end of the horizon as the Eagle, and are ready to transform and move beyond. I was ready for transformation, and it came in as a giant serpent. It reminded me that in my ancestral Nordic mythology, Jörmungandr is the Midgard Serpent (also World Serpent) who encircles the realm of Midgard.

From Wikipedia:

"Fenrir, Jörmungandr, and Hel were living with their mother in Jotunheim, realm of the giants, when the gods of Asgard received a prophecy that they would cause trouble in the future and so Odin ordered them removed when they were still quite young. He hurled Jörmungandr into the sea, consigned Hel to the dark realm of the dead below icy Niflheim, and eventually had Fenrir bound to a rock on an island.

Jörmungandr grew to such an enormous size that he encircled the world – which was envisioned as a flat disc (remember the flat disc) - and held his tail in his mouth.

Jörmungandr is therefore understood by modern-day scholars as an agent of transformation along the lines of the symbolism of serpents in many if not all of the belief systems of the ancient world. Cultures as diverse as those of Egypt, Mesopotamia, and many others frequently feature a serpent as either an adversary of established order or an integral aspect of it but, either way, as transformative entities.

His name is pronounced your – mun-gander (also given as Jormungand and meaning "huge monster" or "great beast"), and he is one of the oldest entities in Norse mythology...."

Shamanism, mythology, religions have all seen snakes and serpents as dark transformative beings. Even the shadow work that we are doing is a form of rejuvenation on some levels as the snake cannot grow if it does not shed it's skin. Just as the caterpillar can't fly if it doesn't become soup. Every change in our state of being or consciousness, requires a shift from old to new, past to present.

In ancient Mesopotamia, the god Ninazu was the serpent son of the healing goddess, Gula. She carried a staff entwined with serpents. He and his brother, Damu worked transitioning souls from life to the afterlife. All exponential growth is about physical changes. Even as I went through my life changes, my physical body changed.

Again, Wikipedia reminds us that:

"There are many examples of the serpent-as-transformative-agent in cultures around the world, but probably the closest to Jörmungandr is Apophis from ancient Egypt. Apophis (also given as Apep) was the Great Serpent who tried to kill the sun god Ra every night in an effort to plunge the world back into primordial chaos and undo the work of order established by the gods. The Barge of Ra sailed across the sky all day from dawn to dusk before diving below the horizon into the underworld."

If we think about the Barge of RA, we have the being, RA, the soul, and the navigator or possibility, mediator, and life path. In my divorce the mediator was a beautiful navigator in my journey from one life to the next.

We can all dance with the serpent if we are ready to undergo a transformation of our emotional self that finally allows us to reach through our fears to embrace our soul path. The Serpent is the experience of the Barge, and in this aspect, it is like our breaking free from the cave in order to see the Aurora Borealis, which signifies truth to me. They light that stems from our heart.

The double symbolism used by the Feathered Serpent is attuned to the dual nature of the deity. Both of the Cosmos where being feathered represents its divine nature or ability to fly to reach the skies, and of the Earth being a serpent representing its human nature or ability to creep on the ground among other animals

The creation of this new you, the new mind, and the new creative heart brings that duality in where you are both more intuitive, but also able to be in awareness of what next physical step to take. Like the shedding of your skin, you are healing your aura, revealing a golden and beautiful new you. Perhaps this is what it all was for me, as the next book is about the golden new world.

Within you has always been the Cosmic Serpent. Just as we started with the Draconian codes, we have come to the connection of heart and mind. Your mind is always communicating with the genetic, or say epigenetic, code of the heart, and these epigenetics are the heart of our life. Your consciousness and subconscious mind are always planting seeds within the third dimensional or Middle World "you". You were always changing, but perhaps just not yet aware.

SOUTHERN CROSS

When people think about shamanism, they often go right to the etheogenic properties of the plants that are worked with. The ayahuasca, psilocybin mushrooms, peyote and other medicinal and hallucinatory plants. If you have read about my journey into shamanic practice, you know that you only need to go into your mind to create the same aspects using what I call, "imagination meditation".

In my aromatherapy book I have a chapter on the plant spirits, but this is the core of where herbology comes from. If angelica is supportive of our breathe work, it is then believed as a plant spirit that life was breathed into the roots, and its spirit was awoken like a birth. When we prepare it through cleansing and anointing, maybe even turning it into tea or an essential oil it is the creation of ritual at the core. The founders of Aromagnosis say that angelica *"reaches across the realms seen and unseen and connects matter and spirit like a vast spiritual ladder. It has a powerful presence and its hollow stem symbolizes this ladder. It fills the spiritual body with a golden light and hugs the heart. ... Gently reminding us that we are loved, and that negative thought patterns, emotions and self-doubt aren't who we truly are."*

This is the medicine for the harmonization of head and heart. It is the support that we often need to go home. These codes are coming through the light grids, that golden light, that is weaving your soul truth of where you came from, into where you are. This is the creation of home. It is this essence that comes to us through the Eagle, that which can see further than our own eyes, to bring us the messages that we need.

When we are living in our centered home, the seeds we plant are our soul seeds, and as starseeds they are creating the home that will cosmically create a different future for all. This is the highest good. This is what Thomas Kinkade was sharing when he talked to me about the seeds of our heart. What you have hidden in the darkness of your heart, in the cave, is the beauty that the world most needs. Set it free. Those that come through your teachings, your gift, as we all came through the Soul Space of the magical black hole that brought us to the light of our world, are the legacy of the light field. This is our calling.

Evelyn Rysdyk is a Nordic tradition shamanic practitioner. I dreamt that she was sitting at my table and she says that she doesn't do tarot readings for everyone. She pulls the overall energy of the 4 of Thorns (swords). Then she pulls the Ace of Cups and the Hanged Man and asks me what is going on with my life, so I tell her.

She then gives me a rock, and as she hands it to me, she notices there is a bump on my chest. She squeezes it like a zit and out pops a crystal that she says was anchoring me into this stagnant space. She tells me to hold onto it because we are going to release it properly. I wake up and it is 6:30 AM and both of my ankles (the backs) hurt.

Why am I feeling Inflexibility and guilty? Just weeks ago, I shattered my world into many pieces in order to align to my truth. Being in our true identity, shedding our skin and growing can show off lingering energy that was stagnating on the surface. Our ankles represent the ability to receive pleasure, as well. For me pleasure has to be connected to the emotional heart space, and change is difficult whenever it has to do with intimacy and childhood attachment patterns. Our ankles and our knee chakras are very tied into our Fire center. Yes, my pride was hurt because I wasn't being accepted for this beautiful growth stage of life. Pride and ego stem from the same part of the brain where intuitive messages come from, but these were encoded by our ancestral mothers to keep us from surrendering to the will of the Supreme Consciousness. In other words, they didn't want us to starve or be eaten by dinosaurs. This push and pull had me angry, and yet it was still old sacral stories.

Water in the knee indicates a holding of emotional energy, especially a resistance to surrender, as there may be too much emotion to cope with and the weight is being carried in the knees. Surrendering to my emotions has been hard to do. I realize that I have never felt that I could be who I was, always maintaining the Jesters role.

I went into the journey space to find this heart stone. I was shown that when we stopped talking, I packed my heart with salt and calcium to block the physical pain. This heart stone is clearing that old pain away in order to live this more open and vulnerable life.

I was then in the space with my Divine Heart, and as I dropped into the earth, they grabbed my hand and I thought they were trying to save me, to keep me with them. But they came with me, falling all the way in. We entered their heart space, which was like a dark bat cave and the Eagle came and took them while leaving me. I said that it would be okay. When they returned, they had a lion's face and walked with me.

We arrived at the shamans' Priestess fire and we were told to put our arms into the fire together. My masculine energy and their feminine energy. When we brought them out, we each had a stone that was a piece of our heart. We rolled them onto our chest and then when they were set in place, I blew theirs into their heart and then they blew mine into my heart. We faced each other. We were wearing cloaks and masks. We took off our hoods and masks and this is where the journey ended.

The truth is at this point I am not in contact with my Divine Heart outside of the energetic space. But collectively I have seen the energy of this new Lion being born. Today I was shown that it doesn't matter how hard the resistance to the new masculine energy is, because the masculine energy has been reborn and will grow in strength. This is uncharted territory, but the record keeper says it is time. Ceres enters Leo on July 23, 2022. 8-8. Eight days in July, and 8 days in August which bring us into the Lion's Gate Portal. Important because we have to listen to our hearts. It is echolocation, as we are relying on the vibrations while we are in a disconnect to the light.

Welcome to your higher self. This is one of your three souls. Pollinate the world around you they say, and yet I feel utterly lost. I have lost a sense of joy and don't know if I can reclaim it.

I try to journey and I step up on this lush green grass between the two green mountains, but this time I am a giant. As I look closer it is not that I am truly a giant, but I am walking through the land of the fairies. My leaving them behind walking into a puddle is perceived by their point of view as I am walking away into the great ocean.

Perception is everything when it comes to our hearts, because perception comes from the limbic brain and can perceive fear, anxiety, disease, and more. I am looking at the Star Rigel as it is working with Mercury. We have just left Gemini season. This star is a blue star, so we are talking to a planet that rules communication.

I am shown a Hopi Kachina Spirit Doll. It starts talking to me of the masculine stepping forward in their energy of Celestial Warrior. So, this walking forward is a mirroring energy. We are in union which only means we are now working in tandem.

This path forward requires them to open their energy to communicate with the divine feminine. I am shown the left foot of Orion, where Orion is called by the Sumerians, URU AN-NA, meaning "the light of heaven." Their name for the constellation Taurus was GUD AN-NA, or "the bull of heaven." And we know that the Star of the Swan is part of the Orion constellation, which is divine feminine energy. As well, Rigel is really a star system composed of three stars, the three souls that have been turning up were created here. Rigel is surrounded by a shell of expelled gas, protecting the codes that formed our trinity.

As I continue walking forward, I am aware I am walking in the path as the masculine energy. If we are focused into the heart space, we can see the path we each walk now energetically. The masculine is seeking the Lion's Gate, looking for the purification of the fire. This is the Hopi Kachina, Toho, the guardian of the northern direction. I have been working in the South, and so there is the illumination that will lead us to the north, soul purpose, North node. I believe the masculine energy is working backwards through the karmic release, moving to the illumination to shed their old skin.

Toho is associated with the color yellow, which is an essence of warmth in this cold element. Reminder that the Hummingbird is also northern and pollinates the summer harvest. Today is the Summer Solstice as I am on this journey. Toho takes on the hunt, very protective over what is his, but is also a healer. He is often represented by a naked man wearing a mask, whiskers, and yellow feathers upon either side of his head to look like the lion's ears. His Spirit reminds our masculine energy to persevere, clarify goals, and move forward to achieving dreams. The Masculine has been wearing a mask, and Mercury means to shift this.

The 28th keeps showing up in my energy field, and 28 August 2022 is important because Venus will be Conjunct Saturn while he's in retrograde. Secret lovers working together for union before the Full Moon in Oct 2022. Fixed Star Rigel will be at 16 Gemini (the Lovers) for seven months through the Full Moon in Aries 2023, which could be very important for those deciding to start their lives together.

I was shown the Divine Masculine energy as the unicorn walking over the small crater on the moon. I see there are several messages here. First that the Divine Masculine is acting as a satellite system looking at what happened in the past to determine what is being mirrored here today. The small moon crater after being scanned collapsed in the real-world version of this event, creating a tower. Whatever has happened was a tower moment. This masculine energy was trying to walk very carefully over this crater, but something conjuncted this energy creating the collapse of their structure and the tower rose.

Part of this is just a reflection of what is happening to the masculine structure in our global world where the feminine is not going to allow their energy to be taken and instead are planting these craters that will be imploding the masculine system.

They told me to look at Aquarius. It was now 28 days ago when I started channeling these messages, and that meaning has a huge impact for me as that was my collapse and quantum death leaping into my new structure. Aquarius, the wish fulfilled.

R. Aquari is a binary star system containing one white dwarf star that has run out of fuel, and one Mira pulsating star that is very slow in its pulsation over 387 days.

So, 28 days ago as they turned their focus to R. Aquari what the researchers saw was not only that it was in eclipse, but that the two stars were at the closest distance to each other that they have been. This only happens every 43.6 years, 13, Rebirth and the number I have given to Ophiuchus energy. It is the Divine energy of birth and creation, and the masculine energy of the Emperor all bound up together.

What they witnessed was the Mira star giving stardust to the smaller dwarf star. And visa versa. The white dwarf takes in the most from the glowing Mira.

Interesting enough, this was where my note taking app created a break. Mirroring the real-world aspects just as a reminder that separation also has a place in your journey. This is all happening on what I thought was Day 827, but was actually day. So, the unexpected Wish was the new Emperor being born. The old cascade is is still trying to hide and resist the New Lion, which is the Wish confirmation from the last video I had recorded. This is what needed to happen in order for our collective wish to come into the reality in our 13th Kundalini life container. Pulling stardust and energy from the active kundalini planes into the 13th life container was never going to happen without a little magic.

Mira means bitter in Hebrew. In Sanskrit, however, it means 'ocean', 'sea', 'limit', or 'boundary'. The masculine in setting boundaries created a bittersweet Tower. It was due to the spiritual energy gifted by the feminine.

Because we see the other meanings of Mira which are "mother earth "peaceful", "amazing", "beautiful", "peace", "prosperous", "helpful", "soft like velvet rose", "princess". The feminine was being spiritually helpful. In the showcase of another aspect of the yin and yang energies between the two.

I am reminded that this exchange happened when it was meant to. When we stop forcing energy, the energy exchange happens naturally.

I am also shown another Mira. This Mira, designation Omicron Ceti, is a red-giant star estimated to be 200–400 light-years from the Sun in the constellation Cetus, the record keeper. I am taken back to that emotion of being abandoned and being "something in the way" that came into my latest Ophiuchus channeled message. A wound that was not seen that needed to come to the surface and be healed. The giving up of oneself and there are so many layers that all of us may resonate with there. Interesting the name of this fiery star, right? We may not believe that the last several years were meant to happen, but they were. The cycle of this Mira is 330 days. 33 to 6, the year of 6. Mira Ceti changes its brightness from third to ninth magnitude over that period of 330 days. 3 square is 9. 3 x 3 is 9, but also times zero is nothing and everything all at once.

Blue is given the classification of the letter O. There are 12 (half of 6) semitones, and 13 is gifted as the sacred sound, as the scale has 32+1 (equals 6) pure harmonic tones and the reference frequency of 256 Hz (13 as rebirth). This frequency beats four times per minute, four being the sacred number of elements, seasons, etc. They say to me Cetus 256 Hz. You were tuned to your sacred frequency in the womb, which is why you know with such a powerful truth what is meant for you. The record keeper holds the true tone of the current timeline.

The letter O is the fourth vowel which represents breathing. First breath of life!! You are now alive again. These years remind you POWERFULLY of this fact. As the 16th letter it was again just confirming that this / these towers were needed and planned for this divine timing. The numerology of O has been seen as both six and seven. This is death, this is birth, this is divine love that was always meant to drive and speed up your soul purpose. Listen to 256 hz in a purity of singularity for 13 minutes four times over the next day and you will renew the connection to your path confirmed by the tingling in the bottom of your feet as you start listening.

The Mira companion in this Cetus binary is a faint bluish white star. I am reminded that Rigel and Vega are also bluish white stars.

Just 16 years ago, pre-shadow of this tower, when I gave birth to my daughter who would be my navigation system to my path (what a blessing she is to me and the world) Mira shed material into a cometary tail 13 light-years in length. The length and timing of the rebirth of the Divine energies coming together. When she was 13, I was awakened.

The Heart Star has shared the understanding of the importance of Dec 2019 which was a different kind of death for us. This was when we gave away our attachment to the old heart of the progressive movement from the 11-11-11 Portal. Our connection to 11-11 had to be shifted. 11-11 is old programming. January 2020 Saturn was forcing our self-awareness personal revolution, but Jupiter kept expanding the possibilities. February 2020 is when I was pushed back from the Capricorn energy of my being and moved early into my Aquarian soul purpose of sharing my channeled messages with the collective.

We have forgotten over the last several years to bless all of these emotions. Collectively the ask for less emotions is drying up the planet. Please bless all emotions that surface to you as they are a gift.

This again all truly started in 2011 with the 11-11-11 Portal. We moved through the portal over that month exiting into the timeline that was changing the 11-11 to the energy of the 12-12 with the Lunar Eclipse on 10 December 2011 is at 18º Gemini 10'. We have the Eclipse with the Sun opposing the Moon, made a T square to Ceres, and the Moon was quincunx Venus. Moon was also on Rigel on Orion, and the Sun opposition comes from Sabik in Ophiuchus. This had to happen to wake you to this higher connection. The South Node was also conjunct with the Moon, illumination that the past timeline and the lower divine partnerships were over. 11 years ago, today I moved back to Seattle, which is where I was meant to be for this to happen, six months before the shift of time would happen. I shifted my daughter's homeschool classes six years later, which brought everything into another perfect alignment. My Spirit guides have given me the number of 6 years to be with my Divine Heart. I don't know if that is six years total, six years more. I just am reminded it will happen as it is meant to happen.

As a final message the Divine Feminine energy must see that the happiness of the Divine Heart in their companion star is essential to be happy together. The Divine Masculine energy is learning that the happiness of others does not come above the happiness and love they have for themselves. The more we love ourselves the better we can love each other.

As I journeyed last night, I was again taken to the Lion who was protecting it's inner or new child. Are we protecting or unwilling to heal and move ahead?

The Hummingbird is the beautifully adaptable animal totem of the North. Our soul guidance system that follows the light through the winter. With this guidance we are always able to adapt our path towards light. Yes, the shadow of the Hummingbird is the Bat.

Bat in the darkness stops looking for that which it cannot see. In the darkest of nights Bat listens to the vibrations using echolocation to find the path. The echolocation cones from the heart transposing what is being said via the soul. It is fear that doesn't want to grow up. It is the fear of the old guard that believe we cannot evolve. But the young Lion cannot remain a child. Our world moves forward and the passage of the old Tower falls into death and is reborn via the release of that karmic lesson. Follow the stars.

I am reminded of the Star of Bethlehem. Before the birth of Jesus there were nine great earthquakes, the last one happening 92 BC, another 11 pointing us to the mastery. This hit the area I've talked about when I was taken to the tomb in 1500 BC. This is where the "Sea People" had hidden the knowledge. Knowing what would come it was moved away to Glastonbury and the area was wiped clean by the tsunami that followed. The ideals were kept in the inner chamber of the Second Temple, but the Arc was already moved, too, when it collapsed. That dark inner chamber was only a space for leaning into the frequencies, and the Bat says that those frequencies remain within all of us through our starseed encoding.

I woke up the next night at exactly 12:12 AM. I had asked for a sign that my inner messages about 1212 were correct. And another confirmation of the Lion's Tomb messages, and the awakening in Israel. The light lies in our hearts. The heart is spoken softly by the feminine. The sound roars out of the Lion's mouth. The masculine is calling the new Emperor to rise out of the darkness to return home. The stars are calling. The Divine Hearts have to find their voice. This is what the Bat in the darkness brings us. Lights are no longer enough. Now is the time of frequency that only the heart can hear.

We cannot hear the approach of asteroids, sort of like the Prius that sneaks up on you and almost runs you down. So how are asteroids like the Bat? They are a shadow of hibernation. In 2012 samples taken of asteroids that were returned to Earth provided new evidence of an extraterrestrial origin for half the planet's water. This is what I was talking about in terms of Jupiter and Saturn working together both to clean up celestial debris, breaking apart large killing machines and sending what is needed onward. Without this tag team, we wouldn't have the tools for life on Earth that we do. July 25, 2019 these two were pointing to the Scopion, warning of the upcoming death. We didn't listen. We're listening now.

All of this is bringing me back to Thuban and the King's Chamber. In December of 2020 Jupiter and Saturn aligned in the Christmas star. We are at the crossroads, the Heart of the Universe, and the council is about to adjourn. They aren't even sure how to save us from the November completion. Between 11-11-2022 and 12-12-2022 is what the council believes is our own making. December 12th the Moon will Square Uranus, which just happened on June 17th. This was day 807. There is something about September 1 2024. Uranus stations and turns retrograde on September 1, 2024, at 27° Taurus 15′ Rx and will push us into inner transformation. On day 807 there was an inner fear of "I can't do it on my own." Being broken by the energy of platonic spiritual love. Here we are, collectively. Broken away from the foundation of friendship, and upending what we know in terms of love.

The Holy Grail started coming to me in these journeys and I could feel that it was all about the state of the Divine Feminine and just being tired of the way that they are not valued. Under the Void of Course Moon yesterday, when no planet is impacting the energy of the moon, I felt free. That freedom was overwhelming and I felt so tired. It was a moment of letting everything go, letting myself just be me. The Moon and the monthly cycle are all tied together, even in our language.

We came from water, and the seeds of who we are reside in the heart, in the emotions, and are always being impacted by the Moon. In the Yin-Yang of Pisces, we see the masculine seed and the feminine seed coming together to dance in that harmonization. This is not just the idea of the sperm and the egg, but this is the vitality of the energy that is in our surroundings, and within ourselves.

One of the signs I find the most joy in looking at their symbol is Aries, who is the warrior, the masculine, the Emperor; and yet this means "Eve". Look at how much the symbol looks like the vagina, the cervix, the uterus, the fallopian tubes and the ovaries. But what is the controller of the Divine Feminine waiting for? The only one that they will accept. The sign of Taurus looks to me like the sperm trying to enter the Egg. But what we know now is that the Egg is the one that chooses the sperm, not the strongest sperm that survives. In IVF the Egg doesn't have as many choices, and yet it still chooses.

Egg, Cosmic Egg, Golden Womb, Creation, the cosmology of what expands out of breath. The Serpent in Greek mythology protects this creation. In Egypt it is the Golden Egg, Ra, laid by the Ibis (the Soul in the Barge), and Thoth, the Higher Self, gifting this to the World. You are the gift of the light, and you are something magical. We often talk about the soul being the essence of who we are, and yet it is the mediator of what is our truth. I love that Thoth is the ruler of the Moon, and yet gifts the birthing of the Sun. Thoth means, "he who is like Ibis", and this is aligned because the light of the Sun is regulated by the Moon.

If all men are born free, how is it that all women are born slaves?
—Mary Astell (1666–1731), considered the first English feminist writer

We are working in the ancient medicine of personal empowerment. That personal empowerment is the Holy Grail of the healer's path, and it is about the reunion with not just the soul spark, but the Thoth. Together the three souls have the ability to heal our separation between our sacred energies. It is time to align our personal vortex, which brings with it infinite abundance, reprogramming of our cellular resistance, releasing the old karmic stagnated obstacles, raising our awareness, and reclaiming what we were chosen to do. Will you receive your gift? Will you reclaim your Golden Egg?

We are talking about the alchemical harmonization of our personal ancient channel of self and oneness. This is where the Merkabah grids, running through your kundalini planes, encodes the soul archetypal energies through the soul waters into the life container. Sound like something we just talked about?

The Holy Grail is the Feminine, the uterus, that which old masculine energies wish to control. That is why fertility weakens. Feminine will not be controlled and birth will become non-existent in the terms of the contract moving forward. This is important in terms of bats. Bats copulate before they move into hibernation and then can hold off ovulation and fertilization for months. They are telling me the Holy Grail has the same ability. If a woman stops ovulation, she stops fertilization. The Holy Grail being the last blood, the Feminine will control the world if they control their ovulation. We are moving into a distinct hibernation of the population. Duality of gender fluidity at the forefront. Fluidity being the energies of our inner masculine and feminine essence. Learning to transform all of this is a battle of head and heart, and it is time to forgive and heal where we haven't expressed our Holy Grail in alignment to our energetic self/soul.

If we start with that breath energy, which is Spirit in life, the root of "spirare", it gravitates to our own magnetic and electric body fields. Like the light is aspected by the planets and directed by the Moon, and the clarity of spirit. Our energy of the breath being of all of the atoms is both masculine and feminine, and it facilitates the action of processing, creating, exchanging energy, and remains in action throughout our illusional life.

Your breath work is the bond to all that was, and that will be. It is how you find and interact with the identical and oppositional atoms, and it is the essence of the wheel, the chakana, the four directions, the sacred work that we do while we are engaged with and working with the ancestral lineage. Here you bring the material and cosmic elements into the work of life. Without breathing we are not alive, but we cannot breathe without connecting to the atomic world of all of that creation. Breathing is the energy of birth.

As we move through this energy of the twelve kundalini chakana points of access, each works both metaphysically and physical embodiments. As they are coordinated into the life container, they teach us how to process the etheric into a transformation of bodily nature.

So, let's look at the elements and cosmology. You know of Earth, Wind, Fire and Water, and/or North, South, East, and West. In the Shamanic approach we have the Condor, Serpent, Jaguar, Hummingbird. In science we have hot, cold, wet and dry. All of these ideas can be seen in the cosmology of the sacred wheel or chakana. The Chakana is the cross within, it touches and moves the wheel, as well. It is our compass of who we are, who we've been, and who we will become. In the constellation, the Southern Cross was the ancient calendar, and aligned to the Tree of Life with the twelve points of the kundalini energies. The center of the hole in the Chakana, to me, is that 13th triangulated life container of the kundalini that I always talk about. As the Maori have called it Te Punga, or "the anchor", it is indeed where we anchor into the body to journey through this life.

The idea of the world being a sphere, or the circle of this container being a sphere, is no coincidence. In the 5th Century BC when philosophers analyzed the lunar eclipse and could see how the shadow of the Earth played on the Moon's surface. As philosophers tuned into a greater understanding of physics in regards to our existence, Aristotle determined that there was no such thing as a void in space. All things, he stated, were combinations of these elements. Each quality can be seen in opposition to each other. Water when cold is ice, and when heated becomes steam. He determined that the heaviest energy was Earth, our center. Then water, which makes up most of the earth and our personal bodies. These are the two of the terrestrial world. The coldness of the wind and the fire of space measure as lighter and make up the celestial realm. Wheel in the sky keeps on spinning.

There was a photo put up by Nasa in April of 2017, and it showed the dark reflection of nebula IRAS 12116-6001. The brightest star in the image was Epsilon Crucis, which is the fifth brightest star in the constellation Crux. Epsilon Crucis was named Ginan, which is its Australian Aboriginal name. This star represents a red dilly-bag filled with special songs of knowledge. The story is that the Mulugurnden (the crayfish) found this as they were bringing the red flying foxes from the underworld to the sky. The bats, those beautiful night pollinators, flew up the track of the Milky Way and traded spiritual songs to the Night Owl (Sirius), named Guyaru. As the bats continue to pollinate through the constellation Scorpius, they traded songs as they go. Their journey is to Crux, the Southern Cross.

These songs inform the people about initiation, which is managed by the stars in Scorpius and related to Larawag (Epsilon Scorpii,). This is all very ceremonial, and is about the beauty of the shamanic council. Larawag is an orange giant star in the Segments, and the stars of the Segments rise and set over the course of about 3 weeks. The Segments represent the exoskeletal segments in the tail of the Scorpion, and I talked about the Mira tail earlier. The tail to me represents our body, it is the Earthly form that we take, coupled up close to the Earth like the image of the Serpent. And the record keeper reminds me that if we attend to our healing, we are in unity like the Whale's tail, which is very powerful and keeps us on the right path.

I am told of an ancient journey of the souls from the ancient Lemuria using the Star Compass. When the distance from the top star in Crux to the bottom star is the same distance from that bottom star to the horizon about 6 degrees, you are at the latitude of Hawai'i. I am told that this was a very important navigational path for the ancients, but we cannot see it fully with the changes in the sky.

Like the Chakana, the Star Compass has four main houses, out of thirty-two houses in the full circle. The four main houses representing north, south, west and east are:

Whitinga – east where the Sun rises out of the ocean

Tomokanga – west where the Sun returns to the ocean
Raki – to the right of the Sun's passage through the sky
Tonga – to the left of the Sun's passage

Each quadrant has seven houses that further divide the horizon with each house replicated in each quadrant. This was helpful to memorize star position and paths. The names of the houses and their meanings are:

Rā – the Sun
Kāinga – where the Sun lives
Ngoi – a land bird (the brown noddy) used by navigators to find land
Manu – the waka as a bird flying across the ocean
Ngā Rangi – the heavens are where we get our clues
Ngā Reo – the navigator listens to the voices of the stars that guide him
Haka – the void where there are no clues, where the true challenge begins.

As always there are pairs, as Southern Cross stars Gacrux and Acrux when they cross the meridian at the same time point south. This happens when the Southern Cross is upright. So, we are always going to be in union, working in tandem, sometimes working on karmic past energies, and sometimes working on dharma of the soul.

My guides told me to look at the Pointers, Na Kuhikuhi, as Thoth and Ibis, pointing us to Crux. These two stars are Beta Centauri, and Alpha Centauri. Alpha Centauri is the closest solar system to our Sun. These two are located in the constellation we associate with Chiron, our wounded healer, Centaurus. Half human, and half horse, which most of us see when we think of the sign of Sagittarius. If Sagittarius is the rebirth, then Chiron is the energy of our being tugged and pulled between these two worlds. One of the soul essence and one of the illusioned reality. These two stars are there guiding us, like Ibis and Thoth, to remember to use our compass as we navigate these paths.

As Crux moves from upright to the horizon, it points to the Crow, Corvus, who's swords' edge is so sharp that it can cleave atoms in two. Sitting just ten degrees off Libra, the Crow is the Sword energy of the Queen of Swords. This is the High Priestess energy, the knowledge that we have sitting so close to our Divine Feminine heart.

I love that Apollo raised Chiron, and taught them how to be the healer that they are. Apollo sent Corvus to fill the cup, the Holy Grail, but he took a long time waiting for the figs on the tree to ripen. Divine timing is not just a thing that readers and gurus talk about, it is written into the mythology in an alignment to our true stories. When Corvus returned in order to not get in any trouble he brought back a serpent as well to say that I was late with the water because the Serpent was in the way. Of course, Apollo was not fooled and instead was angry. He tossed the crow, the cup (Crater) and the serpent into the skies where Corvus seems to always be without the Water or emotions to fill that cup. Crater, which looks like a goblet that is often hard to see, and the constellation Corvus sit on the back of poor Hydra, the water snake.

The Raven, or Crow, points us to Spica, which is to me the seed of the heart and our true abundance. Spica, in Virgo, marks the Ear of Wheat shown in the Virgin's (Hermited Empress) left hand. The left is feminine energy. Spica can see Leo and Regulus from where she stands On Nov 28th 2011 the fixed Star Regulus moved into the sign of Virgo after 2160 years in the sign of Leo. This marked the time of the awakening. The time for the Empress to teach the Emperor through the energetic energy to put aside ego and dispense personal glory. This was timed after the 11-11-11 Portal and the following December Lunar Eclipse.

Spica, is actually two stars that are so close, and orbit so quickly around each other, that their mutual gravity distorts into that Egg shape. They say the pointed (feminine) ends of these egg-shaped stars face each other as they whirl around. These two stars are individually indistinguishable from a single point of light, even with a telescope. Some like it hot, and this is the energy of the Divine Hearts. Your Divine Feminine Energy clings to each other, and in a way the Masculine Energy protects it. You are two, that are one, and you are the Cosmic Egg. These are both dwarf stars that are brightening near the end of their lifetimes. You did not find each other now because it wasn't time, it again was divine timing. It is the fifteenth brightest star, both the obsession, and the Lovers. The sixth is our journey, and we chose it. Arcturus, the lonely star, points to Spica to show the Divine Feminine and Divine Masculine what loneliness is, as that is a possibility. You may find your Cosmic Egg and yet never feel strong enough to allow yourself to be physically together. Arcturus, the Hierophant, is the knowledge that always resides within you. Loneliness is our choice but we do not choose that from our hearts. The aloneness of Spica comes from fear and from in the mind, which is very much where Virgo commands from.

Arcturus is often called the Bear Guard. If we think in terms of tarot, I have been shown the bear as the symbology of mostly the Queen of Pentacles, but I can also see it as the King. This is the guard of the energy where we love ourselves enough to provide for our stability and happiness. It is only after we have found that love of self, that we can share it with another. Beyond that it is all karmic. You cannot reach the Two of Cups, unless you first fill your own cup into overflow. Ace of Cups always comes first. Love is within you, and it was awakened, filling the void in the chakana. Filling the void in your illusioned reality. You have known the spark of this Divine Heart, and you will not forget that love. You can walk around with an empty compass, or you can fill it with your heart's desires. Crux has guided you here, but you have to be the one to drink from the cup of love.

On July 1st Venus will be so close to Aldebaran in the morning, it will appear as if it is forming a second eye for Taurus the Bull. It is time now to see from the heart and mind in harmony. As well the first week of July in Hawai'i, all five planets that are visible to the naked eye, Mercury, Venus, Mars, Jupiter, and Saturn will be in the sky at the same time at around 5:00 AM according to the Hawaiian Star Compass. July will be the last month this year in Hawai'i where they can see the Southern Cross in the early evening sky. At the same time, the summer starline, Mānaiakalani, will be rising in the eastern sky. Māui is preparing to pull the large fish from the ocean, the masculine energy that has been emotionally underwater for most of this year. Again, Mānaiakalani, is in Scorpius, and the tail symbology has been weaving in and out of our codes in the light field of these stories. I feel that there will be three weeks of intensity for our masculine energies. As time is fluid this is all happening when it was meant for you, and when you are reading this remember that.

This is being driven by Mars, and the power of rebirth. Mars will be entering Aries from Pisces on June 27 and will remain there until Aug 10, 2022. Saturn is also moving to Capricorn in its retrograde journey on July 12, and so I feel like that Supermoon on July 13, 2022 will be powerful.

♏

HEAVENLY LLAMA

We had to find comfort with ourselves yesterday with Venus and Mars supporting each other in that trine energy.

Today is a small palindrome 01/10 and it js telling us to go back to the beginning to complete our forward motion. With Orion's Hare (Empress energy) smack dab in the center of Messier 79 we see that the current reality is still being devoured as each world has experienced before us. Behind the hare are the brilliant blue stars, our past, Bluerays, gathering in the core for this big quantum leap forward.

On 01/11 the Green Comet activated this portal in the Southern Celestial Pole. This is very important because of the collected sacred star people that are still deeply involved in the work of the Cosmos. Using Gamma Aquarii, the center Wish and the Lucky Star of Hidden Things, we can see the individual work called for to go into this Portal, with a challenge to have faith that returning to the beginning isn't the same as repeating a cycle. Instead, this is called, birth.

Phi Aquarii pulls on us as it's evolving through the portal from water to mass. It uses Neptune's energy. Neptune first attunes the star portal on January 11th as it is passing 6' due south. South the direction of Sachamama, the Serpent, Ouroboros, snake eating its tail, repeating infinity, we're shedding the past to renew again. By Jan. 20, Neptune sits 12' due east of the same star, now attuning it to the new frequency of the lovers. East the direction of Tata Inti, Father Sun, Eros, Creating Anew. 6 degrees apart we're initiated alone, and at 12 degrees we're attuned to reunion.

There's an opening in the wall that will allow the green comet to activate the exit portal of the Bayer family ring of constellations around the Southern Celestial Pole on 2/2. The first goodbye to the Green Planet, Earth. The lucky star sits roughly 222 light years from our current Earth world.

This is a once in a civilization event bringing in the opening to shift into the long portal to the Age of Aquarius starting in 2024. The final big push into the Great Awakening as we move into this dimensional shift in time & matter. Prepare for some mind-blowing discoveries over that year within the "tunnel to the future".

This song by Chevelle, *Endlessly*, rang through my mind as I was channeling this message ... the specific lyrics I heard over and over again were:

'This silent sulking time is up
Unearth a movement to breathe in full
'Cause this depends on his demands
To seize a moment of fear within

Ten times we've gone down that road

All
This
Time
Felt slow

We're alone
Underground
Where we'll grow
Endlessly"

There is of course more to the song, but there was this conversation that was developing between that which is growing outside of our perception, and the diversion of the third dimensional time that we hold so close to our hearts.

So much of the underground growth that we are working through in these codes, are already designed in the cosmic tunnel of our path. Beyond our basic genetics, we are being recreated in every moment based on the environment surrounding us. Epigenetics, the moment to moment version of genes being turned on and off, and these things that were always encoded, just in case. Who we are, and what we are revolves around these elemental forces all around, underneath and above us.

I was drawn back into a poem I had written just before moving to Seattle the first time, as the karmic purge was so close to the surface of my energy field. This one in particular, "Crucify My Love", seemed almost to be the manifestation of my future, calling for that which was buried to awaken and break through the dirt. But timing, my loves, timing is everything. Divine timing is not in our hands.

"Crucify My Love"

You saw me walk into the water
Without the knowledge will I swim?
It doesn't matter I must follow you
I guess I'm just my father's sins

You touch my spine and pull me closer
You touch my skin and pull me in
I never knew what I was missing
I never knew that I could live

You feel the heat of my desires
I crave your passions, as it feeds my needs
Little death there's never sorrow
You're the temptation I can't leave

Under water, I felt you breathing
I felt my life drift from the flow
Like I was baptized inside your essence
Line up my crosses and I'll bear them whole

Crucify my love
Inside the darkest nights
Crucify my love
Within your tomb I die.

-Barbara Lindahl-Christensen

This... is a conversation of our souls. You're being called, and you're calling out, and the single most important question is, will you answer?

So again, we are being returned to the Southern Cross, which comes to me today as the Baby Llama, with Scorpius as Mother Llama. She who is my envisioned little death.

The Green Comet (Comet ZTF) will move into view in the Southern Hemisphere in February. Currently as I am channeling it sits at the Boötes border. This, again, is the Divine Feminine Shephard who is guiding the Llamas.

Several weeks ago, the Llama came to my channeled messages in my backyard carrying the Andean mountains. The mountains are both a place of power and powerful healing energies. This morning as I journeyed to the mountains, and I entered this state through the very tree that had become the Llama in my yard.

As I entered it was quite dark but I was able to find my way to the door. Exiting I found myself on the mountain, walking down a path in the forest under the Full Moon lit night. Surrounding this Moon was the Yana Phuyu (dark clouds). It is in the dark spot between Scorpio and the Southern Cross where the Llama, or Yacana, lives at the center of the celestial River Of Life. Her eyes, called llamacnawin by the Incas, are its only bright part. She who sees. May 5th at 10:33 PM PST, the moon will be full in Scorpio as a Lunar Eclipse, opposing Uranus. I expect this is where I was led as I walked down this path into the dark clouds.

As I followed the Moon, *Mamakilla*, she showed me the shadows as I felt fully grounded but was walking now on air. I arrived at the Moon, and Mother Spider joined me today as the Dark Tarantula, the reincarnated soul of the Warrior. This is extremely important to me, as I have been working with the Warrior part of my being that has not only protected me in trauma, but deters me from opening to emotional vulnerability.

Mother Spider starts spinning webs first around my throat and then on specific energy centers around my body, eventually anchoring me to this Moon. She sits across from me and says, "You're anchored to a part of yourself that is still in orbit. It is far enough away to be held at a distance, but close enough to impact you." I saw this part of myself as a toddler, but it was specifically the Divine Masculine energy that I let die as I went through a soul trauma. At that moment in time, I chose to only let the toxic remnants of my masculine energy remain within reach.

The purest part of my Divine Masculine energy came and sat across from me, and smiled gently. He said, "It was your choice to let me go, but I have never left you alone."

I asked him, "Would you like to be reintegrated into our being?" He did desire this. Mother Spider had me lay down, and he stood and slowly lowered into my body like one layer being placed into another. As we started to morph into one, Mother Spider wrapped us into her silk. Victor Manuel Ortega-Jimenez and Robert Dudley of the University of California Berkeley found that spider webs change their shape in response to the electrostatic charges. The webbing was charged differently to this new frequency, binding our energies together.

This is when the Eta Draconis, three golden stars, reappeared to me. They had said to me a few days prior, "Triad". Our primal triad is woven into our natal chart. This refers to our Sun, Moon and Rising signs. In religion a Triad refers to a grouping of three gods. So, this was talking to us about the way the Golden Ratio is spiritually grouping us together with Divine Timing in every aspect of this grid of light.

March 2022, Mars, Venus and Saturn were high in the night sky sparking a passionate transformation. Divine Feminine and Divine Masculine hitting their limitations of the containment of knowledge. War, fire, heat, or chaos was determined to be the only way to break open this life container for one with greater capacity to grow.

I had started channeling with the new world, specifically through the Golden Starseed Council. We are awakening from a dream, yet are still dreaming.

dream /drēm/

a series of thoughts, images, and sensations just before awakening

This was a dream.
Was it??

Another from my first book of poetry released sooooo long ago...

'Rain – Words of Self, Life and Devotion"

The 12th, divine lovers, ascended healers ... You feel it as we are being attuned together.

"Can't Change Your Spots"

I would if I thought it would make it all true
Wish my shining knight were wrapped up in you
But I know that the spots on the leopard are there
And I know you won't change even though you still care
Into the crack, I turn to steal away
Look through the lens to come watch me play
Over the edge as I dangle my toes
Very sure I am dreaming, and I don't want to let go
Enter my heart through the truth, and come inside
Do it now before I am gone too far to find
Listen to fate as it stares you down square
Alone in this state as you fear coming here
You'll never step forward until you progress
Step out of the comfort, and into the next
Discover the fear that's been holding you back
Hope will draw nearer, and almost attack

So I steal these few moments to hold in my heart
Taking full the risk of falling apart
Knowing you'll never get rid of your spots
I would wish if I thought it would create Camelot.
-Barbara Christensen

Cycles of emotional healing. That is the dream just before you wake. Which dream is real? That will you feel, or that which you see?

The Goddess Cybele, Great Mother, is coming forward to say that this cycle is complete. Now we rebirth. Today, here in Seattle, 65 Cybele (her Asteroid) became visible around 18:42 (MST), 49° above our south-western horizon, as dusk faded to darkness. It then sank towards the horizon, setting at 23:37.

On the Greek Gods & Goddesses (.net) from October 20, 2019 (which is a VERY profound date for me) they say:

"Having fallen in love with a much younger and very handsome shepherd named ATTIS, Cybele fell into a fit of rage upon finding out that Attis had fallen in love with another, a nymph called Sagaris. Cybele showed up to the wedding feast and terrified the guests and Attis so greatly that he fled into the mountains where he fell at the base of a pine tree. In his madness, Attis mutilated himself and bled to death where he lay. Cybele, who came to deeply regret her actions and mourned the loss of Attis. However, JUPITER assured Cybele that the pine tree would become forever sacred. It came to be adopted by the priests of Cybele, the Galli."

Jupiter entered Aries December 20, 2022. (12/20/2022... lots of 2s) Being a fire sign it teaches us to embrace our courageous movement forward as we grow and expand in this time of our life to the next. Jupiter has a very busy year, and it seems to be that way for many of us

Expansion then came into the tarot readings, and Gemini's reading was 22:22 long. Angel's guiding this beautiful movement forward. Within a few weeks I had seen the encapsulated energy of the 3s and the 4s also bring their frequency to the new life container.

Most months I am lucky enough to participate in a women's circle at least once. At the time of this new birth with the Triad, I joined the circle unknowingly about to open up this next code.

Before our circle, I like to pull an oracle card or two. The oracle cards I pulled that morning were Eagle, Summer, and Oracle. I am guided to remember that we must look from a higher perspective because the messages can often get hidden in the work. The honey bee is busy pollinating, and we've all seen those adorable pictures of the pollen covered bumble butt sleeping in the flower. We have to pause, in the work, to gain the most important information.

The bloomeria crocea came to me and is considered to be a member of many families. Which metaphorically is such a beautiful concept. It called me to the dry foothills of California's Baja, and we walked into the sunny pine forests. Everything, as you've learned by following these channeled messages, flows in cycles. The desert was returning. There, in the moment of journey it was blended into the beautiful hues of the other flowers surrounding it. The most striking to me are the blue (bluerays), the violets (indigo and cosmic unknowns) and of course its own yellowish gold hues. I was so drawn to the essence of gold that I had not seen before.

Then the Golden Starseeds came in, and as they spoke to me, yet I could not hear their words, just the vibrations. Sometimes information must travel great distances to land. We have to be reminded to have grace when the messages take longer than we'd like. The council of these elements appeared almost metallic as they spoke to me as separate particles, but speaking through one mouth.

I see the Crystal-Golden children in our reality as those born since the year of the Golden Metal Dragon, which signified the end of the Fourth World and the birth canal of the Fifth. The Fourth World which we haven't even ventured to us already dying in our sense of timing. Here we saw the YOD of Saturn, Pluto, and expansive Jupiter pointing the way in Gemini to union. YOD, the Golden Ratio of Triad, or known in Astrology as G-d. Also, there are those new Crystal- Golden Starseeds rebirthing themselves. You are as new as these babies.

My word that Spirit gifted to me was Solidarity. Soul tribes are unifying, all going through the childbirth of a new humanity together. There will be tantrums, there will be growth and having to let go of that which we want to hold onto. I am reminded of my daughter's yoga pants that became ankle length, then capris and finally a last dawn of bermudas before she could let them go. Some of our states of comfort aren't healthy, and we have to address them as we cannot carry them out of the birth canal with us. Some of our DNA remolecularizing of body, mind and spirit has not been comfortable. Hold strong to each other in hearts and souls. That is our guidance.

I went to a Yurt in the middle of the forest that evening for a sacred initiation of Kabbalistic ritual wrapped into the Candlemas ceremony. I've never felt the kundalini planes so activated as I did in that ceremony. When Spirit introduced me to the 13 planes of kundalini planes (12 that intersect into the 13th) I had never heard of the 13 Elemental Gates. In the teaching of Kabbalah, mystic ancient practices, the Holy Temple would have to bow 13 times, paralleling the 13 gates [of the Temple], to enter or leave the temple.

The Thirteenth Gate.... There is one pathway through which all prayers may pass. Mind blown!! We walked the gates and I felt it. The council came to me in this celebration of rebirth and remembering. In Kabbalah, Yod, is the 10th Hebrew letter, and the number of both completion and new magical action. It is the spiritual belief, the hand of G-d and our Ouroboros. Here in continuity, the unbroken and consistent existence of energy or infinity. On the 10th the transmission from the light council of the Fourth World started to land. It was so long ago that Chi Draconis had opened our inner activation of the Fourth World, but timing is irrelevant to this new world. It doesn't exist.

Proxima b, or as they are calling her, Minerva, has been with us all along. We call her the Owl, High Priestess, Athena, Empress, even Divine Feminine. She is the 6 degrees (4.2 light years from Earth) one of the Triad, the triple star system, Alpha Centauri. We're being tugged apart by our celestial mirror to be rebirthed, but it comes ever so deeply through our personal Chironian death. Jupiter has been the birth canal. Juno is the awaiting partnership that the reunion of the two has created. And Minerva, the new birth of knowledge. My personal Juno was Sextile Jupiter at 3 degrees, and Conjunct Neptune at 6 degrees at my natal birth. And my Juno placement is Scorpio, death. There also resides my Pallas and my Ceres. Thoughts and Love (Queen of Cups) are the G-ds of Triad with Death in my old life container. Interstellar Owl who connected me with Jupiter and Venus last year. She awaits her Union in birth, Juno.

So where is Juno now? Asteroid 3 Juno is currently in the constellation of Cetus. The current Right Ascension of Asteroid 3 Juno is 01h 11m. Angel number 111, what you've manifested all along. Don't think I don't also see the irony of the number six showing up there. Cetus, of course, is the Record Keeper whom I always see as the Divine Masculine Whale.

Last year when I worked with Jupiter and Venus in creating my special talisman it was a special day and time crafted by a master shamanic Astrologer. On March 11th there will be another amazing day as the waning gibbous moon will be 10 degrees of Zubenelgenubi (Zubenelgenubi and Zubeneschamali are considered to be the brightest Libra stars, yet were once the Scorpion pinchers) and at 11 degrees Spica. A waning moon invites our surrendering to the softening heart and mind. Libra having been created as the balance of the day and night, equally shining the light and dark matter of the situation.

On this date we're being reminded that the "balance of Heaven" only exists due to the severing of it from Death (Scorpius). Libra, brings the birth and the death, and in thus morning pulls the Ear, Spica, out of the hold of Death. We are opening to hear something special as Venus and Jupiter are within 10 degrees of each other until 2025. Expanding the voices of the heart, Jupiter has been slowly moving through Cetus and Venus enters Cetus on February 21, with 21 being The World card in tarot. What we can't see from our viewpoint is that Alpha-Centaurids meteor shower just passing its peak in the Southern Hemisphere. But Jupiter and Venus can see it. They are together watching, and Spirit says, etching everything into the records. A cycle ends, and the birth canal softens.

On February 22 we have a triple conjunction of the Moon, Jupiter and Venus. The number 22 being important as the number of being between the end and the beginning.

Mānaiakalani, in Scorpius, has attuned us for our cycle change, and again on March 11, Mars will be dead center of Taurus' horns. Mars driving our birth from the Crown Chakra of the Divine Masculine. Just before we hit this event, thirteen days before which is very significant to the Death and Rebirth card in tarot, Pleiades will conjunct the Moon. In Celtic tradition Pleiades is symbolically associated with the cycle of death. As Sirius is seen as the Spiritual Sun, the brightest star of Pleiades, Alcyone, is our Spiritual Moon. The emotional and thus physical Moon in conjunction with our higher self, Spiritual Moon, is bound to cause some serious shifts. The spiritual feminine energy will be felt so strongly in this birth canal that the emotions may finally break through the wall that has stood between the masculine and feminine energies.

It is at this point that Mars passes Beta Tauri, who is both the tip of the Bull's horn, but the heel of the Charioteer. We are being birthed in the breech position, bringing in special powers of healing to the divine, and a powerful sign that you are not following the traditional path! Mars will not pass Beta Tauri again until August of 2024. When this happens, the Moon will be in Taurus, and Sextile with Saturn in the waning gibbous phase. I am told this will be the effacement of the birth of the Age of Aquarius. The birth of the new age most important pushes happens between October 13 2024 and November 07 2024. Passing the Gatekeepers through the last gate of the Karmic purge. The awakening cry heard around all dimensional paradigms happens November 15 2024 as Saturn again turns direct in Aquarius and our new age finally moves forward in continuity.

Starting in January 2023 Saturn returned to Aquarius after thirty years. Spirit is laughing at the humor that the Lord of Karma will keep us waiting through 21 months of dancing with Aquarius before we truly come into the new age.

What is dying, is starting now. I saw Wolf, again, holding the feminine hand as she was breathing her last breath in. She was both Earth Goddess and the feminine sacrifice. I saw her in the Pawnee buffalo hunt as they awaited the timing of the Morning Star. This year the Morning Star comes into June as Mercury, with Jupiter's watchful eye. During the nine days the Sun and Mercury sit in conjunction in Taurus. This is the Divine Masculine embodiment of the sacred cosmic heart.

These Pawnew, named for the wolf spirit, knew that it was Wolf's death that brought death into the world, and today Wolf stands with the final sacrificed woman as she fades. June 13th through the 15th during the triple conjunction, the Moon moves out of the ending of Pisces, 12th House, into Aries, 1st House. By June 21st we have the Solstice entering with the triple conduction of the Moon, Mars and Venus, and the Moon has taken up protection in Cancer, 4th House. Here the people, the land, and the ancestors are released to change karmic debt into something that can grow into a beautiful new energy. This allows Wolf to finally be set free.

The next day I viewed this breech turning around and the head and shoulders were out of the womb. And as we do, it offers us and expansive new direction of the divine union with Jupiter. As the aurora borealis or Northern Lights and aurora australis or Southern Lights came through the 'From The Diary Of Woo' as the electrical connection of the lovers, Jupiter's four major moons (four angels, four directions) have aurorae at visible wavelengths that we can now view.

I've written before about the brain and the fingerprint connection. Now Michael Levine, a developmental biologist, in his research has amassed much evidence that the embryo, in this case tadpoles, are molded by bioelectrical signals. These particular signals emanate from the young brain long before it is even a functional organ. So, we are being created for the frequency or we aren't created at all. No bioelectrical current, then no brain. No brain, then no life prints. It is an interesting study.

Scorpius has been called the Rival of Mars, and we see that reflected in the houses as Scorpio is Death in the Eighth House ruled by Pluto, followed by the shedding of the womb, Ophiuchus who did not get a house, and then the Rebirth on the 9th House of Sagittarius who is ruled by Jupiter.

Ophiuchus without a house is the Ouroboros and comes in after death to empty the old container, shed the past and start a new layer. This is why we needed Saturn at the end of the journey with Capricorn. Saturn comes in to that Capricornian

10th House to regulate things and do it all by the book. Aquarius, the 11th House ruled by Uranus breaks through the long labor to open up the portal of life. However, the bioelectrical connection of the Yin and the Yang in the 12th House with our highest heart of Neptune is truly the most important step in our birthing process.

When we reach Aries, the First House, which is ruled by Mars, who comes out screaming having already done this a thousand times before, we are already aligned to a higher purpose that we drive our entire life towards. Your life container has only eight houses. We scream coming into light, we breathe and our heart beats, and they stop and we die. This explains a lot about the Kundalini planes as they've been described to me by Spirit. The other four are part of the transmutations process in a timelessness of death and birth wrapped into the Ouroboros, or the Infinity loop, and electrically embedded as our neo-cortex in the womb. It is no wonder the early Babylonians saw the Scorpius as having a human torso, and the Aztec as half-man and half-scorpion, as well.

So, you've reached an especially important time of birth now. Humanity is divided as those after the "seven" year will unwind their karma, and those that have shed it. The Cosmic Aurorae, the new four directions of expanded human consciousness. The Ancient Chinese texts saw Scorpius as the Azure Dragon that rises from the Celestial River. This dragon, or serpent, takes up a quarter of the sky. The Heart of the Dragon can be found in Scorpius, where it is marked out by the bright red supergiant star Antares. if you're moving on the expansion, this heart is the cause of your awakening. Blame it in the stars.

The Azure Dragon eats the Sun, time. So, the ancient dragons of the Green World are teaching them new lessons. Dragons who sometimes sit stubbornly, are being taught the new codes. They know the time is drawing near. An ancient timing that could be any length. I cannot say. However, the dragon's mouth is open and its tongue is already extended.

If these stars were the beginning of our death, and this rebirth, then these moons or Galilean satellites have been tracking us all along. Galileo Galilei discovered these moons in 1610, in tarot Spirit says, "The tower of completion."

Ganymede, carried off by the eagle to serve as the water bearer. This moon shows us the new direction of Life, the Sun, the East. Only open hearts ready to share their emotional being can be born here.

Lo, the volcanic South, tugging apart our barrier of self as we shed the hold to the old material plane. Lo, the Goddess of love being turned into the white calf. We must give and receive love to be protected on our journey forward. This heart has wandered this earth, crossed the deep sea of emotions, swam the path of the birth canal, where the heart was restored to its original form.

We were given information just too days ago while I was editing the book that Venus' volcano, Maat Mons, was active and that activity was captured in 1991. This eruption on Venus at that time was similar to what was released by the 2018 Kilauea eruption in Hawaii. Those dates may be very important you the journey of your heart path.

Europa, the Ice Queen of the West, illuminations, having been disguised as the White Bull, but prophesied as the White Buffalo can now fully emerge. Only the illumination of love will bring her to light. The White Buffalo Calf Woman returns at the end of an age, and we are almost to the New Age of Aquarius. She brings spirituality and highest love, and she told us that when all four sacred white buffalo had returned, the people would be at a crossroads, and if they took the right path, there would be a renewal of the Earth. This is the path to the Fourth World, what remains in the Third World will be vastly destroyed.

And of course, our North Node, soul purpose, Callisto, which others may see this union and its path as ugly. Tarnished by the barrage of wounds over four billion years, this heart moon is still the most beautiful space that will ever be. In mythology Callisto was placed in protection of the Great Bear. As the virgin love, Callisto shows us a love like none that ever existed before. She who sacrificed, and was hidden, this heart is a reunion before we can enter the Fourth World.

It all comes back to the current North Star of Polaris, sitting within The Bear. This channeling has led us full circle as a way to show that this quantum leap is just a new cycle of life, although different. I am reminded that this current Spark was started in June 2013 when Jupiter sat conjunct to Fixed Star Polaris.

On January 29th of this year, that beautiful Green Comet sat on the tip of Polaris inviting us to follow your true North Node. It was heading to that very powerful Full Moon on February 5 2023 into Capella, which wits in the overhead constellation Auriga. This constellation is only visible in its entirety as far south as -34 °. Another confirmation of the year of seven, to me. This is that Charioteer that we are seeing so often in our readings these days. Would it shock you to learn that Capella is actually a group of four stars? It is, of course, considered the sixth brightest star in our Earth's sky. So hard to distinguish from Mars due to Capella's yellow-orange appearance. This leap takes a lot of faith, while letting go of the old stories and letting go of the reins, and letting the Universe drive. Does the Universe drive you towards death? Of course, in every meaning of the word. All stages of the wheel are always turning never to run over the same speck of dirt again.

Four... everything that Scorpius opens up. The four levels of the life container preparing us for birth. The four stars that reminds us of our heart's path forward. The four moons that show us the ascended energy that has always awaited us.

I finally see The Hermit in truth! This is Ophiuchus holding the container that time exists in. Outside of your Green World, it spins in a way we cannot even understand, but it has always known and been a part of you.

Here this Spark ends and when read you are fully attuned to your Celestial Codes. You can come back, re-read, gaze and meditate with each symbol to find even more embodied codes to weave into your new frequencies of gold. Golden, like the hardened fiery magma rivers deposited on Venus' surface from other dormant volcanoes. All of the codes will awaken again. Just as we've found a giant plume of magma forcing its way up through the Mar's mantle, that which goes through death will yet be reborn. Love is never ending, and our journeys together are folded into many dimensions and timelines so that we are reliving the awakening again and again with the hope that divine love never truly dies. It only ever ascends.

ABOUT THE AUTHOR

Barbara Christensen is a gifted intuitive medium, that channels Spirit to bring clients a diverse approach to wellness. She is a successful author, holds a diploma in nutrition and created the *Paleo Vegeo* lifestyle movement. Barbara holds certificates in fitness, various energy modalities (*reiki, quantum biofeedback, Access, shamanic*) and is both a Certified Aromatherapist and aromatherapy teacher. She has been working with individuals and business owners for over two decades using her unique talents to bring clarity and wholeness into the lives of others

Barbara Christensen is also the creator of the YouTube channel, Mindset Unicorn (Be Light Create LLC), where she creates unique tarot readings using the akashic records, shamanic healing, Spirit guides and a variety of inner knowing energies to decode and enlighten the human experience of the soul's journey. Barbara works with mirror souls to bring healing in and create the destination that both souls are working towards in the often described "twin flame" union.

"Working with the energy of the Universe is within us all. The secret is to open your mind to explore the truth of who you are. We are all rainbows made up of star dust!"
- Barbara Christensen

The Shamanic Approach is the idea that within each of us lives a shamanic self. This self is the keeper of the fire within the community. That community could be just you; it could be your family; it could be an organization or the clients you work with. Usually, it is all of the above. As the keeper of the fire, you must nourish yourself and care for your being in order to serve the purpose you have here on this earth. We each carry a purpose that was coded into our genetic hand prints and fingerprints months before you were born. This was done to make sure you could later find your path when the life journey takes you off the path of your desired destination.

The Shamanic Approach means you aren't just given "answers' or "the secret pill" that will fix everything. Barbara works with her clients in a way that allows you to be held within a guided space, and then within that sacred space you are taught to do the work yourself. That is the only way we unwind the karmic timing to get back onto our destined journey.